PHILIPPA PEARCE

A Dog So Small

ILLUSTRATED BY ANNABEL LARGE

PUFFIN BOOKS

PUFFIN BOOKS

Published by the Penguin Group
Penguin Books Ltd, 27 Wrights Lane, London W8 5TZ, England
Penguin Books USA Inc., 375 Hudson Street, New York, New York 10014, USA
Penguin Books Australia Ltd, Ringwood, Victoria, Australia
Penguin Books Canada Ltd, 10 Alcorn Avenue, Toronto, Ontario, Canada M4V3B2
Penguin Books (NZ) Ltd, 182–190 Wairau Road, Auckland 10, New Zealand

Penguin Books Ltd, Registered Offices: Harmondsworth, Middlesex, England

First published by Constable 1962
Published in Puffin Books 1964
Published in this edition 1995
1 3 5 7 9 10 8 6 4 2

Text copyright © Philippa Pearce, 1962
Illustrations copyright © Annabel Large, 1995
Afterword copyright © Elaine Moss, 1995
All rights reserved

Typeset by Datix International Limited, Bungay, Suffolk
Set in 12/15pt Monophoto Bembo
Made and printed in Great Britain by Clays Ltd, St Ives plc

Contents

ACKNOWLEDGEMENTS

The quotations on page 65 and page 69 are respectively from *The Dog Owner's Guide* by Eric Fitch, *Dogs in Britain* by Clifton Hubbard, and *About Our Dogs* by H. Croxton Smith. The author also acknowledges indebtedness to Cordelia Capelgrove.

CHAPTER I

Early on a Birthday

*T*he tapping on the window woke him. He was fast asleep, and then wide awake because of the tapping. Perhaps the pigeon always began as early in the morning as this, for it was certainly always tapping when the boys woke. But that was usually much later, with full daylight and with the smell of breakfast-cooking coming from downstairs.

Cold, scentless, dim was the early morning, and Paul and Frankie still lay sleeping. But Ben had woken at once, and at once he could not stay in bed a moment longer. He got out and went to the window. 'Pij,' he said softly through the glass; but the pigeon knew that this was not the boy who gave the food, and moved doubtfully off to the edge of the window-sill. The sill was always white with pigeon-droppings, so that Ben's mother – who did not know of the daily feeding – said that the bird was an obstinate creature that did not know when it was not wanted; but it did.

The sky was a dirty pinky-yellow where dawn over London fought with the tired light of thousands of street lamps. The birds were awake – pigeons, sparrows, starlings; but nobody was in the street. It lay empty for Ben; and he could not wait a moment later in bed – in the bedroom – in the house. With action he must fill the space between now and breakfast time, when the post came.

He dressed quickly and left the bedroom. The other two were still sleeping, and the pigeon had resumed its tapping. He crept out on to the landing. His parents were still asleep: his father snoring, his mother silent. As soon as Mrs Blewitt woke, she would begin a little rattle of cups, saucers, teaspoons, tea-caddy, teapot, and electric kettle. When the tea was made, she shook her husband awake. And when his snores had ceased to buzz through the house, you knew that the Blewitt family had really started its day.

Ben passed his parents' door, and then his sisters' – more warily. May was talking to Dilys. May was still half asleep, and Dilys three-quarters, but that did not matter in their kind of conversation. May, the eldest of the family, was going to marry Charlie Forrester early next year, and Dilys, very close to her in age, was going to be her bridesmaid. So they talked of weddings, and wedding-presents, and setting up house with a three-piece suite and curtains with pelmets and a washing-machine . . . 'And a wedding like a newspaper photograph, with a bridesmaid and a page,' said May, going back to her favourite beginning. Ben was tiptoeing so carefully – so slowly, that he had to eavesdrop. They spoke of the prettiness of a page-boy to carry the bridal train; and they wondered if Frankie, being really still only a little boy – although not really pretty any longer, and he might need some careful persuading to the idea . . .

Frankie? Ben's eyebrows went up; but it was none of his business, this morning of all mornings. He tip-toed on, down the stairs and out of the house. He closed the front door behind him with care, and then said quite loudly, 'It's my birthday.' The pigeon came to the edge of its sill for a moment, to look down at him, nonplussed. 'Ah,' said Ben, looking up towards it, 'you just wait and see.'

He said no more, even to Paul's pigeon, even in this empty street, and even so near to the time of his birthday post. His grandfather Fitch had promised him – well, as good as promised him – a dog for his birthday. That was some time ago, when Ben had been on a visit to his grandparents. Grandpa had been watching him play with their dog, Young Tilly, and had suddenly said, 'What about a dog of your own, boy – for your birthday, say, when that comes round?' He had spoken from behind his gnarled hand, because

Granny was there, and she missed little. She disapproved of dogs, even of Till. So Ben had only breathed his 'Yes' to his grandfather, and Mr Fitch had nodded in reply. But surely that had been enough.

Grandpa would have to tell Granny in the end, of course, to get her agreement; and then he would have to get hold of just the right kind of dog. There might be a delay, for there would be need of delicacy and discretion. All this Ben had understood, and he did not alarm himself that his dog was not mentioned in the weekly letters to his mother. Grandpa wrote the letters at Granny's dictation. She would have written them herself, but she had arthritis and could not use a pen properly. So Grandpa wrote for her, very slowly and crabbedly. Granny told him what to say, first of all about the weather and then about the rest of the family. Old Mr and Mrs Fitch had six surviving children, besides Mrs Blewitt, and all grown up and married and with children of their own. By the time Granny had finished with news of them, there was no room for talk about dogs. Moreover, Grandpa hated writing and by the end of each letter his fingers were cramped and exhausted with the effort of holding and subduing the pen. All this Ben told himself reassuringly, having faith that his grandfather would neither forget a promise nor break it.

For months now, Ben had been thinking of dogs. As long as you hadn't been given any one kind of dog, you had a choice of the whole lot. Ben had not bothered to be reasonable in his imagining. He had had

Alsatians, Great Danes, mastiffs, blood-hounds, borzois
. . . He had picked and chosen the biggest and best
from the dog-books in the Public Library.

This morning Ben was making for the River – some
way from his home, but worth the walk. Looking over
the parapet, you had the only really extensive view
possible in this part of London, and that was the kind
of view you needed when you were thinking of a
really big dog.

He turned out of his side-street into another and then
into a main road. There was very little traffic yet, and
he made the street-crossings easily, with only a brisk,
almost absent-minded look in both directions. Already
his mind was leaving London in the early morning for
Dartmoor at night. Over that wild, nocturnal waste
the hound of the Baskervilles was silhouetted against a
full moon low in the sky. The dog's spectral eyes dwelt
upon the figure of Sherlock Holmes. . .

But a boy couldn't *do* much with a bloodhound,
unless there were criminals loose. Not a bloodhound
then, this morning. The road along which Ben was
trotting rounded a bend and came within sight of the
bridge over the River. This was the point at which the
Blewitt family still sometimes revived the old, old joke
about Ben's littleness. If he grew to be six foot high,
Ben sometimes thought, they would still make that
joke. For from the other side of the bridge towered up
Big Ben.

Ben Blewitt was still thinking of his dog. An Irish
wolf-hound perhaps – but they looked so unkempt and

terribly sad in the photographs in the dog-books. If he were dealing with wolves, he would really prefer a borzoi . . .

The traffic crossing the bridge into central London had been very slightly increasing all the time, and the number of pedestrians. Ben was outpaced by a man in a bowler hat and dark suit, carrying a briefcase. He had walked from Tooting and was going to his office in the City, where he liked to be at his desk by half past eight in the morning. He did this every morning – he was not a married man.

He passed Ben on the bridge, and went on to his work; but Ben stayed in the middle. He laid his elbows along the parapet and gazed over that amazing length and width of water, here in the heart of London. The only buildings to interrupt the expanse were the bridges, and they put only their feet into the water as they strode across.

This was what he had come for. The expanse of the River reminded him conveniently of the enormous expanses of Russia, the home of the borzoi. At school Ben learnt about Russia – what Russians choose to eat for breakfast and what agricultural implements and crops they use on which soils; he wasn't very much interested. His father read about Russia in the newspaper, and thumped the table as he read. Paul and Frankie read about Russian space-travel. But Ben's Russia was different from all this. For one thing, his country was always under deep and dazzling snow. The land was a level and endless white, with here and there

a dark forest where wolves crouched in th
to come out at night, howling and ravenin
it was day-time in Russia. Sleighs had been
into the snow, and left. Each sleigh was covered with a
white woollen blanket to match the snow. Beneath the
blanket — but wait: already men on horseback were
beating the near-by forest. Wolves came out. They
were rushing past the sleighs. Men concealed in the
sleighs threw back the blankets and, at the same time,
unleashed their coupled borzoi dogs. Magnificent, magnificent beasts! They leapt forward after the wolves. The
wolves were fast, but the borzois had greyhound bodies,
their whole bodies were thin, delicately made, stream-
lined for speed. The wolves were fierce, but the borzois
were brave and strong. They caught up with the
wolves: one borzoi on each side of a wolf caught it and
held it until the huntsman came up with his dagger —

At this point Ben always stopped, because, although
you couldn't have wolves, he wasn't so keen on killing
them either. Anyway, from the far side of the bridge
the moon-face of Big Ben suddenly spoke to him and
said half past seven. The wolf-hunt with borzois had
taken a long time. Ben Blewitt turned back from the
River to go home to breakfast.

He broke into a run as he realized that the morning
post would have arrived.

CHAPTER 2

A Dog Behind Glass

The stream of traffic was much thicker as Ben hurried homewards. He rushed up to his usual crossing at the traffic-lights, and a policeman said warningly, 'Now then, sonny, not so fast,' thinking he might recklessly try to cross at once. But Ben waited for the red traffic-light as usual. However urgent your business, you simply had to, in London. A cat which did not know about this scudded across the road without waiting. 'Oh!' said Ben, and closed his eyes because he could not bear to look, and then opened them again at once because, after all, he had to know. The cat looked neither to right nor to left, but suddenly quickened her pace as a car flew towards her. Cat and car sped on paths that must cross. 'She's done for!' said the policeman. The car passed, and there was the cat, safe on the farther pavement. She disappeared at once down some area-steps, and Ben thought that when she reached the bottom she would certainly sit down to get her breath back and to count her nine lives. The policeman was shaking his head.

Ben crossed soberly and safely at the red, and then began running again. When he turned into his home street, he saw that the time was late enough for most of the dustbins to have been put on to the pavement. His father was just trundling the Blewitt dustbin out to be emptied in its turn. This was the day of his father's late work-shift on the Underground.

As Mr Blewitt was going indoors, he saw Ben at the end of the street and waved to him to hurry. Perhaps it was just for breakfast, but perhaps it was for the post. Ben tore along.

The post had come, and it was all for Ben. His father had piled it by his place for breakfast. There were also presents from May and Dilys, Paul and Frankie; and his mother and father had given him a sweater of the kind deep-sea fishermen wear (from his mother, really) and a Sheffield steel jack-knife (from his father). They all watched while, politely, he opened their presents first of all, and thanked them.

He was not worrying that there had been no dog standing by his place at the breakfast-table. He was not so green as to think that postmen delivered dogs. But there would be a letter — from his grandfather, he supposed – saying when the dog would be brought, by a proper carrier, or where it could be collected from. Ben turned eagerly from his family's presents to his post.

He turned over the letters first, looking for his grandfather's handwriting; but there was nothing. Then he looked at the writing on the two picture-postcards that had come for him – although you would hardly expect anything so important to be left to a postcard. There was nothing. Then he began to have the feeling that something might have gone wrong after all. He remembered, almost against his will, that his grandfather's promise had been only a whisper and a nod, and that not all promises are kept, anyway.

He turned to the parcels, and at once saw his grandfather's handwriting on a small flat one. Then he knew for certain that something was wrong. They would hardly send him an ordinary birthday present as well as one so special as a dog. There was only one explanation: they were sending him an ordinary present *instead of* the dog.

'Open it, Ben,' said his mother; and his father reminded him, 'Use your new knife on the string, boy.' Ben never noticed the sharpness of the Sheffield steel as he cut the string round the parcel and then unfolded the wrapping-paper.

They had sent him a picture instead of a dog.

And then he realized that they *had* sent him a dog, after all. He almost hated them for it. His dog was worked in woollen cross-stitch, and framed and glazed as a little picture. There was a letter which explained: 'Dear Ben, Your grandpa and I send you hearty good wishes for your birthday. We know you would like a dog, so here is one . . .'

There was more in the letter, but, with a sweep of his hand, Ben pushed aside letter, packing-paper, string, and picture. They fell to the floor, the picture with a sharp sound of breakage. His mother picked it up. 'You've cracked the glass, Ben, and it's a nice little picture – a little old picture that I remember well.'

'I think it's a funny birthday present for Ben, don't you, Paul?' said Frankie; and Paul agreed. May and Dilys both thought it was rather pretty. Mr Blewitt glanced at it and then back to the newspaper he had opened.

Ben said nothing, because he could not. His mother looked at him, and he knew that she knew that, if he hadn't been so old, and a boy, he would be crying. 'Your granny treasured this because it was a present from your Uncle Willy,' said Mrs Blewitt. 'He brought it home as a curio, from his last voyage – the last voyage before he was drowned. So you see, Granny's given you something that was precious to her.'

But what was dead Uncle Willy or a woolwork dog to Ben? He still could not trust himself to speak; and now they were all looking at him, wondering at the silence. Even his father had put the paper down.

'Did you expect a *real* dog?' Frankie asked suddenly.

Everyone else answered for Ben, anyway.

His mother said, 'Of course not. Ben knows perfectly

well that Granny and Grandpa could never afford to buy him a real dog.'

His father said, 'And, anyway, you can't expect to keep a dog in London nowadays – the traffic's too dangerous.' Ben remembered the cat scuttering from under the wheels of the car that morning, and he hated his father for being in the right. 'It isn't as if we had any garden to let a dog loose in,' went on Mr Blewitt; 'and we're not even near an open space where you could exercise it properly.'

'There's the park,' said Dilys. But Ben knew that park. It was just a large, flat piece of grass in front of a museum. There was a straight, asphalted path diagonally across it, and seats set in islands of asphalt. There was a notice-board by the gate with forty-two by-laws beginning 'No person shall –' Eight of these said what no person should let a dog do there; and an extra regulation for that park said that dogs must be kept on leads. But you never saw a dog there, anyway.

May was saying, 'What about the River?' She only thought sensibly on her own subject, nowadays. 'Couldn't a dog swim in the River for exercise?'

Then Paul and Frankie and even Dilys laughed at the idea of Ben's exercising the dog he hadn't been given in the only open space, which was the River. They laughed merrily among themselves. Ben's hands, half hidden by the wrapping-paper that his mother had picked up from the floor, clenched into angry fists. Mrs Blewitt, still watching him anxiously, took the letter again to skim through the rest of it. 'They say they hope you won't be disappointed by their present – well, never mind that – and – why, Ben, just listen! – they ask you to go and stay with them again as soon as you're able. Isn't that nice? You always like that. Now, let's see when you might go . . . Not next week, but perhaps the week after, or perhaps even –'

On this subject Ben had to speak. 'I don't want to go there,' he said. 'I don't ever want to go there again. I shan't.'

CHAPTER 3

The Unspeakables

At the breakfast-table borzois, bloodhounds, Irish wolf-hounds, and all the rest had vanished together, and Ben returned to loneliness. To be the middle child of a family of five may not be as sociable and warm as that central position sounds. Paul and Frankie were much nearer to each other in age than they were to Ben, and so were May and Dilys. The two youngest and the two eldest made two couples, and in between them came Ben, alone. He had never been much interested in the girls' affairs, anyway. Paul and Frankie followed more sensible pursuits, and Ben sometimes allowed himself to play with them for relaxation. But, really, their games, their plasticine, their igloos made of eggshells and Seccotined cotton-wool, and all the rest – these were things he had done with. Even their pets seemed childish to him: Paul's pigeon, Frankie's white mouse, their silkworms, and racing beetles stabled in matchboxes. Ben needed a mature, intelligent creature-companion. Nowadays it always came back to the same thing: a dog.

Because Ben seemed somehow on his own, his grandparents Fitch had often had him to stay with them. They lived in the country in a house so small that there was not room for more than one visitor at a time; and, of the five Blewitt children, Ben was usually that one. And Grandpa had a dog – a bitch. She was called Young Tilly only because she was the daughter of Old Tilly; she was really quite elderly herself. But Tilly was still game for anything. She panted at Ben's heels as he wandered along the driftway that ran by his grandparents' home. He could not say why, but this was what he most looked forward to on his visits: a fine day, and going along, but not in a hurry, a stem of grass between his teeth, and the company of a dog that snuffled and panted and padded behind or to one side, or suddenly pounced into the hedgerow, in a flurry of liver-and-white fur, with the shrill bark of 'A rabbit! A rabbit!' and then came out backwards and turned round and sat down for a moment to get her breath back and admit: 'Or perhaps a mouse.'

All this Ben gave up at that bitter breakfast-table when he said aloud that he would never visit Grandpa and Granny again. After all, he could not. You could not possibly accept the hospitality of someone who had so betrayed faith. In disappointment and indignation he had said he would never go there again. He would not.

Only, Ben's indignation was flawed by a sentence – if you could call it that – at the end of the hateful birthday letter. It had been added by Grandpa after the signature – that is, after Granny had ceased dictating. There was a spelling-mistake in the sentence, which made it certain that Granny knew nothing of the addition, for she always checked Grandpa's spelling. Under Granny's nose but without her knowledge, Grandpa had managed guiltily, hurriedly, urgently, to write a telegraph-sentence of four words: 'TRULY SORY ABOUT DOG.'

Old Mr Fitch had written as he might have spoken from behind that gnarled hand, furtively: 'Truly sorry about dog.' To say so, in such a way, was almost painful – and Ben did not wish to pity his grandfather now.

Ben first knew of the telegraph-sentence when his mother made him read through the rest of his letter, after his birthday. She had also propped up the wool-work picture on the living-room mantelpiece, trying to make the family admire it. Ben averted his eyes; but his father had taken notice.

'We always used to think,' said Mrs Blewitt, following his gaze, 'that the hand in the picture was the hand that did the embroidery.'

'A woman,' said Dilys, for they were all looking at the picture now, except for Ben.

'A dotty woman,' said Mr Blewitt. 'The dog's all right, I suppose, for a dog in wool, and the hand's all right; but the two of them don't go together for size at all.'

'Perhaps a little girl did the embroidery,' said Mrs Blewitt, apologizing for the lack of skill in proportion.

'A *little* girl!' Mr Blewitt snorted. 'Just look at the size of the hand behind the dog! A giantess, I'd say.'

Mrs Blewitt tried to make Ben feel how lucky he was to own a picture of a dog embroidered by a little giantess. 'I said that it was a foreign curio, Ben! Your Uncle Willy wrote on the back the name of the foreign place where he bought it – Mexico, I think.' She took the picture from the mantelpiece and turned it round: 'Yes: "Bought in Mexico, on his third voyage, by W. Fitch."' Then she hesitated. 'And there was something already written on the back when he bought it.'

'Well, what?' asked Mr Blewitt.

Mrs Blewitt simply passed the picture to him, so that he could see for himself.

'Ah,' said Mr Blewitt, after he had read.

'What does it say?' asked Paul.

'Read for yourself.' So the picture went from Mr Blewitt to Paul, then to May, Dilys, and Frankie. Each looked at what was written there, mumbling over it, but saying nothing. The picture reached Ben last because he had deliberately not interested himself in it. But curiosity made him look to see what none of the others would speak aloud. On the back of the picture, in a handwriting older than Uncle Willy's, were the words:

CHIQUITITO

CHIHUAHUA

'It's a double tongue-twister in as foreign a language as could be,' said Mr Blewitt.

Ben still held the picture back to front, staring at the second – and possibly the stranger – of the two strange words. Oddly, in spite of its outlandishness, it looked familiar to him. He thought that he might have seen it in print somewhere, not so long ago. Seen it, not heard it, for he had no more idea than the others how one should pronounce such a word.

'The second word . . .' he said slowly, trying to remember.

'Ah, now!' said Mrs Blewitt. 'The second word was the name of some place in Mexico. I remember Willy showing us on the map.'

On the map – then that must have been where Ben had seen the name printed. Only – only, he hadn't been studying a map of Mexico recently; indeed, he couldn't remember when he had ever looked at one closely enough to notice any names. They weren't even doing Mexico at school.

What did it matter, anyway? He reminded himself that he hated the little picture, as an unforgivable betrayal by his grandfather. Yet, again – 'Truly sory about dog.' He could almost see his grandfather's hand writing that, his fingers clamped round the pen desperately driving it through the curves and angles of the capital letters: 'TRULY −'

'You know, Ben,' said Mrs Blewitt, 'if you went to stay with your granny and grandpa, you could find out all about your little picture. I know Uncle Willy told your granny, and she never forgets anything.'

Ben looked at the picture, but thinking of something else: 'Truly sory −' He saw his grandfather saying it with furtive but true, unmistakable sorrow. He saw his face behind the curved, gnarled hand − his grandfather's face creased all over with wrinkles, and the skin an old red-brown from his working so long in all weathers, mending the roads for the Castleford County Council. His grandfather had blue eyes, and a browny-white moustache that lengthened out sideways when he smiled. He would smile with anxious apology as he said, from behind his hand: 'Truly sorry about dog.'

'You might do well to take the picture with you, when you visit them,' Mrs Blewitt said, growing bolder from Ben's silence. Ben knew that he ought not to let his mother take for granted that he would do what he had said he was never going to do again. But he continued in silence.

Frankie spoke: 'Ben said on his birthday that he never wanted ever again −'

'How often have I told you not to talk with your mouth full?' Mrs Blewitt said swiftly. Frankie's mouthfuls were large, so he would have to chew some time before speaking. Meanwhile, 'You could go next week, Ben,' his mother pointed out.

Now Paul protested: 'But that's just what Frankie was talking about. He was just going to say that Ben said –'

'Be quiet, Paul. Frankie can speak for himself,' said Mrs Blewitt, 'when he has finished his mouthful – of a size he should never have taken in the first place.'

Paul and Frankie had to be silent, but Frankie was on his last chews and gulps.

Mrs Blewitt clinched the matter with Ben: 'So it's settled you go, with the picture.'

'All right,' said Ben; and Frankie nearly choked.

'But, Ben, you said you'd never go there again!' he cried.

'I can change my mind, can't I?' asked Ben. 'And you've just spat some boiled egg on to your jersey.'

'You go straight into the scullery, Frankie Blewitt, so that I can wash it off at once.' Mrs Blewitt shooed Frankie ahead of her, and said over her shoulder to Ben, 'Write now. Say you'll arrive a week on Saturday, by the afternoon express. Grandpa can meet you at Castleford station after his market-day shopping.'

So, the following week, Ben went. He took one large suitcase, containing his oldest clothes for the country, and bathing-trunks in case the weather grew warm enough for him to bathe in the River Say. The case also held a tin of fudge, two plum cakes, and a meat pie, all home-made by Mrs Blewitt. She always sent what she could, because nowadays Granny could manage so little cooking, and Grandpa had learnt so few recipes. In the middle of the suitcase, packed round with socks and handkerchiefs to protect its glass from further damage, travelled the picture of the woolwork dog.

Mrs Blewitt saw Ben off at Liverpool Street Station. Old Mr Fitch met him at the other end of his journey.

As the train came into Castleford station, Ben saw his grandfather waiting with the crowd on the platform. He was carrying a bulging shopping-bag in one hand, and the other held Young Tilly's lead. She was crouching on the platform behind him, as close to his ankles as she could, and peering between them. She disliked trains, and this one – being an express – swooped and roared and rattled up in just the way she most hated.

The train, slowing now, passed Mr Fitch and Tilly, and they both caught sight of Ben at the same time. Mr Fitch began to move, but Tilly was quicker. She dashed out from behind his ankles, found herself over-bold in her nearness to the still moving train, and dashed round to the back of Mr Fitch's trousers again; then she came out as before, but more cautiously. Her movements brought the lead in a complete turn round Mr Fitch's legs. By the time the train had stopped and Ben was getting out, Tilly had lashed old Mr Fitch's legs to the platform and, at the end of a shortened lead, was trying to choke herself and bark at the same time.

Old Mr Fitch could take no step forward, and his hands were fully occupied. But Ben, approaching, saw his browny-white moustache lengthening. 'Ah, boy!' he said. His eyes looked bluer than ever, because he was wearing his best blue suit, which he usually wore only for chapel on Sundays. With a shock Ben suddenly knew that he must be wearing it for *him*.

There was a muddle of leaping dog and lead and suitcase and shopping-bag, as they greeted each other, and then they disentangled everything. They were going to leave the station. Fumbling in his pocket for his platform ticket, not looking at Ben, Mr Fitch said, 'She put her foot down about the dog, you know. But I was truly sorry.'

'I know,' said Ben. 'You told me so.' With his free hand he took one of the handles of the heavy market-bag, and helped his grandfather carry the burden out of the station to the bus.

CHAPTER 4

To Little Barley and Beyond

*T*he country buses started from a special place in Castleford, a place not frequented by town buses; and, on market-day, the passengers were nearly all people like Grandpa Fitch, doing their weekly shopping. A bus crew usually knew its whole load of passengers by sight, even by name.

'Fine day, Grandpa,' said the driver of the Yellow Salden bus, who was leaning against his vehicle, smoking. He knew that old Mr Fitch lived half-way to Salden, by the driftway beyond Little Barley.

'It is, Bob,' said Grandpa. 'Got my grandson with me.'

'Wouldn't know you apart,' said the driver, and winked at Ben.

They got on to the bus. It was a single-decker, so there was no bother about taking Tilly upstairs. She crouched under Grandpa's knees, and on top of them he carried all his shopping and Ben's suitcase, up-ended. Ben himself had given his seat up almost at once to a woman with shopping and a baby.

When the bus was quite full and the driver had swung up into his seat, the conductress called down the crowded gangway: 'Anyone *not* going beyond the Barleys?' There was a hush among the passengers, for this was rather like asking whether anyone in a party had not been invited. 'I –' said a hesitant voice, and everyone turned round or craned forward to see who. A lady with a suitcase and no shopping said, 'I – well, I was going just to Great Barley. The timetable said this bus went to Great Barley.'

'*Through* Great Barley, without stopping,' said the conductress. 'Full and five standing, on a market-day, we don't reckon to set down or pick up until after the Barleys. There's other buses to do that.'

The lady was civilly helped off the Salden bus and directed to a Great Barley one. Then the Salden conductress asked her question again, and a third time just to be certain. Each time there was an unbroken hush. Then she rapped on the driver's window and they set off – the five miles from Castleford to Great Barley, and straight through Great Barley, and bouncing over the two bridges into Little Barley, and through that, and well ahead of time, and everyone looking forward to early teas.

Beyond Little Barley the bus entered real country-side, with shaggy elms at the far limits of fields and meadows on either side of the bus route. A house stood quite by itself at the side of a field-track.

'The driftway!' cried the conductress, in case Grandpa, from behind his luggage, had not seen where they were. But he was already struggling out of his seat, with Tilly and Ben pressing close behind him.

The bus stopped for the first time since Castleford traffic-lights. There was someone waiting to get on, anyway: young Mrs Perkins, who was the Fitches' next-door neighbour.

'I popped in twice to see her,' said Mrs Perkins to Grandpa, as he came down the bus steps. 'She wouldn't let me lay your tea, though. Said she could manage. Last I saw of her was going upstairs to watch for the bus from the bedroom window.'

'Thank you, my dear,' said Grandpa. He and Ben and Tilly and the baggage had got off; Mrs Perkins got on. The driver leaned from his window and said something he had been thinking out ever since his remark to Grandpa Fitch in Castleford: 'All three so alike that I can't tell which of you is the dog!'

'That's Bob Moss!' said Grandpa, as the bus drove off. The driver was laughing so much that you could see the spasms of it in the wobbling of the bus along the road. Then Mr Moss remembered his responsibilities: the bus straightened its course, and dwindled into the distance.

Mr Fitch let Tilly off her lead, and she went ahead of them up the driftway. A little way along it there stood what looked like one house – really, two semi-detached, brick-built cottages that some farmer had put there for his labourers, long before people had thought of building houses where they might easily be connected with sewers and water-pipes, electricity and gas. In one half of this double house lived young Mrs Perkins and her husband; in the other half, the Fitches. The front of the house looked over the road and its infrequent traffic. The back looked up the driftway – a rutted track that ambled between fields and meadows, skirted a wood, crossed the river by a special bridge of its own, and came out again at last – with an air of having achieved nothing and not caring, anyway – into another country road just like the one it had started from.

Evidently Mrs Fitch had seen the bus, for she was coming down the stairs as Grandpa and Ben came through the front door. The front door opened straight into the living-room, into which the stairway also descended. Ben had a rear view of his grandmother in a black dress with little purple flower-sprigs on it. She was climbing down the stairs backwards and very slowly, because of stiffness in the knees. As soon as she heard the front door open, she called, 'Don't let that dog bring all the driftway in on its paws!' Tilly stopped on the threshold, sighed, and sat down. Mrs Fitch reached the last stair-tread: 'I've laid the tea, as you see, in spite of what's-her-name Perkins thinking I'm not up to it any more.' She reached floor level and turned to face them: she was a little old woman, thin, and yet knobbly with her affliction; but like some tool of iron, much used and worn and even twisted, but still undestroyed and still knowing its use.

'Well, Ben!'

Ben went forward and kissed her, a little timidly.

All Granny Fitch's grandchildren felt a particular respect for her; so did her sons-in-law and daughters-in-law, and even her own children; even Grandpa Fitch felt it. He and Granny had been married for nearly fifty years, and they had brought up eight children – not in this tiny house, of course, but in another not very much larger. Grandpa had always worked on the roads, for the County Council, which was a steady job, but not well-paid. On the birth of their first child, Mrs Fitch had discussed the future with Mr Fitch, and he had taken the Pledge – for economy, not for principle. So he gave up his beer, and he gave up his pipe at the same time, and he had always given all his weekly wages into his wife's hands. Mrs Fitch had gone out to do morning cleaning in Little Barley as soon as the eldest Fitch child had been old enough to begin looking after the youngest; and she had managed. People in the Barleys remarked that the Fitch children were cheaply fed, but well-fed; cheaply dressed, but warmly in winter and decently in summer. They had all gone to the village school, where they worked hard – their mother had seen to that. One of them, by means of scholarships, had reached a university; two had gone to Castleford Technical School. One of these had taken a job in London, where she had met and married a young fellow with a good job, working on the Underground Railway. This was Lily Fitch, who became Mrs Bill Blewitt, and the mother of Ben.

In the struggle of bringing up the children, Granny Fitch – for she always took the family decisions – had never accepted charity. Not much was ever offered, anyway, in her experience. You could not call scholarships charity: they were worked for – earned. Now Granny and Grandpa were old, and Grandpa had retired from road-work. They lived on their pension, and that was just enough. They still took no charity, even from their children. They were independent, Granny said; they always would be, unless anyone wanted to make a silly splash with expensive brass-handled coffins, when the time came.

In spite of her arthritis, Granny got about wherever she wanted in the little garden or indoors. This afternoon she had laid the tea-table for Ben's coming, so that Grandpa had only to brew the tea, while Ben made the toast.

Over the tea-table Granny questioned Grandpa – what he had bought in Castleford market, how much he had paid, whom he had met, what they had said. Then she questioned Ben. She wanted to know how he was getting on at school, and Paul, and Frankie. She wanted to know about Dilys's deciding to change her job, and about May's getting married – and, of course, all about May's Charlie Forrester, whom Granny had met only once: was he really sober? was he steady? was he hardworking? was he helpful about the house? Grandpa, unobserved, took an extra spoonful of sugar in his tea, while Ben answered briefly, carefully, accurately, saying he didn't know if he didn't know, for all this was what Granny liked.

After tea old Mr Fitch usually read to his wife, whose eyesight had dimmed from much plain sewing when all the little Fitches had had to be so cheaply dressed. Granny had the choice of Grandpa's reading from the Bible, the Chapel Magazine, or any recent family letters. Grandpa read as haltingly as he wrote, so he gladly gave up his task to Ben this evening. There were two letters to be read: the first was from one of Ben's aunts who had settled in Essex, and the other was from an uncle in Canada. As Ben read, Granny would occasionally stop him to call, 'Do you hear, Joe?' and Grandpa would come out of the scullery, where he was washing up the tea-things. Then his wife would repeat to him the news of the letter, in the very words of the letter, for Granny had a remarkable memory for things both near and long ago. Each time, Tilly – from her position just outside the open front door – would whine a little, hoping that this meant the end of the reading. Every time she did so, Ben whispered 'Tilly . . .' in a steadying voice that promised her his company later.

When he had finished reading the Canadian letter, Granny said, 'Would you like the stamp?'

'Well . . .' said Ben, not liking to seem ungrateful. 'I

mean, thank you . . . But, as a matter of fact, I have – well, really, I have those Canadian stamps, so if you don't mind –'

'Answer what you mean, boy,' said Granny, and the end of her knobbed forefinger came down like a poker-end on the table, so that Grandpa in the scullery jumped, and Tilly, who had been crawling forward until her nose rested on the threshold, winced back.

'No, thank you, Granny,' said Ben.

'Not interested in stamps now?'

'No.'

'But in dogs?'

'Yes,' said Ben, quickly and truthfully because he had to, but unwillingly.

'Disappointed you didn't have a live dog on your birthday?' The clash and splash of washing up stopped in the scullery. Ben was silent too. 'Answer,' said his grandmother.

'Yes,' said Ben.

Again, a silence. Then Granny: 'What possessed Joe to promise such a thing . . . Do you know how many grandchildren we have?'

'Twenty-one.'

'Supposing your grandpa and I began giving them all a dog each – twenty-one dogs . . .'

Grandpa appeared in the doorway of the scullery. 'Not one each. One to a family.'

'Seven dogs, then,' said Granny.

'One's in Canada.'

'Six, then.'

Grandpa went back into the scullery, having reduced the number of dogs as much as was in his power. Ben could see that, even so, there were far too many dogs. He couldn't have had one. He began to tell his grandmother that, anyway, you couldn't really have a dog in London. But Mrs Fitch was continuing her own line of thought: 'And I hope Lily'd have more sense, too. A dog eats bones that would make good soup, leaves mud on the lino, and hairs on the carpet. Yet men and children – oh! they must have a dog! It beats me why. Look at that foolish Till!' Young Tilly knew her name, but knew the tone in which it was spoken; she groaned hopelessly. 'We have her,' said Granny, 'as we had her mother, because she's said to keep down the rats and catch rabbits for the pot. But there never have been rats here, and there aren't rabbits any more; and, anyway, she's too old and fat to catch anything except a bit of bacon rind sneaked down on to the floor.'

Grandpa, with the tea-cloth in his hand, came right out of the scullery, and spoke with fire: 'There aren't any rats because she keeps them down all the time; and it's not her fault if there aren't rabbits any more. And stout, not fat.' He went back into the scullery before Granny could reply.

'Well,' said Mrs Fitch, 'that is something your grandpa and I shall not agree about. Ben, will you put the letters away for me, please? With the others, in the top drawer in the chest in my bedroom, on their right piles.'

Ben had done this before. He went upstairs to the

deep drawer that held all the letters from Granny's children. They were divided into eight piles, one for each son or daughter. He recognized his mother's handwriting on one pile. One pile was much smaller than the others, because it had not been added to for many years; the postmarks were all foreign, as the stamps would have been, of course, except that they had been cut out long ago for grandchildren who were collectors. These were the letters written by Uncle Willy, who had been drowned before he had had time to marry and set up a family – Uncle Willy, who had brought the woolwork dog from the place with the unpronounceable name in Mexico.

Ben put the two latest letters into the drawer and shut it, with a sigh for the dog he had been cheated of. Somebody sighed in sympathy behind him. He turned. There was Tilly. She was never allowed upstairs, and one would have thought that she could never have conceived the bold possibility of a dog's going up there. But, as she waited on the threshold downstairs for Ben's coming, she had seen the hedge shadows lengthening along the driftway, and had smelt the end of the day coming. She could not bear that she and Ben should miss it altogether. Grandpa had come out of the scullery and Granny had then engaged herself in a one-sided conversation on the worthlessness of dogs. Taking advantage of this, Tilly had slid into the house and upstairs, to find Ben.

Ben took her great weight into his arms and staggered downstairs, to where a window opened on to the back garden. He dropped the dog through the window and went down to his grandparents.

'I've put the letters away. Can I go out now?'

'Yes, be back before dusk,' said Granny. 'I expect you'll want to take that dog.'

'She's gone from the door,' said Grandpa, looking. 'But no doubt you'll find her outside.'

'I'll find her,' said Ben. He stepped outside, into the early evening sunshine and the smell and sight of flowers and grass and trees with clean country air above them up to a blue sky. He dropped his eyes from the blue and saw Tilly's face round the corner of the house. She advanced no further, but jerked her head in the direction of the driftway. 'Come *on*,' her gesture said.

Ben picked a stem of grass growing beside the porch, set it between his teeth, and followed her.

CHAPTER 5

Life With Tilly

*I*t wasn't that Ben wanted to live in the country – oh, no! The country was well enough for holidays and visits, but Ben was a Londoner, like his father. Mr Blewitt was an Underground worker, and, as the only English Underground was in London, Mr Blewitt could no more live out of London than a fish could live out of water. Besides, he liked London; so did Ben.

Ben liked to rattle down moving staircases to platforms where subterranean winds wafted the coming of the trains; he liked to burrow along below London. Above ground, he liked to sail high on the tops of London buses, in the currents of traffic. He liked the feel of paving-stones hard beneath his feet, the stream-ing splendour of a wet night with all the lamps and lights shining and reflected, the smell of London. After all, London — a house in a row in a back-street just south of the River — was his home; and he had been called — so his father said — after Big Ben.

But he would have liked to have had a dog as well.

That was why Ben particularly enjoyed his country-visits to his grandparents. During a stay, Tilly became his. This was her own doing, and was done with delicacy, for she became his companion without ceasing to acknowledge Grandpa as her master.

Grandpa gave Tilly's care over to Ben. He made her dinner — kept an eye open for all rinds of bacon, for bones, and other left-overs including gravy, added dog-biscuit and a little water, and stewed it all up in Tilly's old enamel bowl on the kitchen-range. He combed out her spaniel curls, dusted her for fleas, gave her a condition powder — did everything. He shielded her from Mrs Fitch, who knew perfectly well that there was a dog about the place, and yet never allowed herself to become reconciled to the fact of it. Ben picked up Tilly's hairs whenever he saw them indoors, rubbed her feet on the doormat before he let her inside, and walked between her and his grandmother when they entered together. Young Tilly herself knew how to evade notice. In spite of her bulk — 'a back made to carry a tea-tray,' Grandpa said — she could move so lightly that there was not so much as a click of her toe-nails on the linoleum.

Tilly was with Ben, whatever he was doing. On the first days of his visit, he spent most of his time about the house and garden, helping Grandpa. He kindled the fire in the range, fetched the milk from the milk-box at the end of the driftway, pumped the water, dug the potatoes, fed the fowls, and gathered the eggs. Always Tilly was with him. They spent one whole afternoon with Grandpa, helping to knock up a new hen-coop for a hen with a brood of very late chickens. The chicks ran over Tilly's outstretched paws as she dozed in the sun to the beat of Ben's hammer on the nails.

On other days they were more adventurous. Granny directed Grandpa to pack a lunch of sandwiches for Ben, and he went out after breakfast until nearly tea-time – with Tilly.

They went down the driftway. Once – in spite of everyone's saying there weren't any more, nowadays – they started a rabbit. Tilly threw herself into the chase, ears streaming behind her, until the rabbit began really to run. Then, intelligently, Tilly stopped.

Once, in a copse, they started a squirrel; and Tilly would not believe she had no possible chance of catching it. She thought it must fall.

Once they found an old rubber ball in a ditch: Tilly found it and Ben threw it for her, and they only lost it hours later, in a bed of nettles.

The weather became hot, and they bathed. Just before reaching the driftway bridge over the Say, they would strike off across marshland to the river. Tilly led the way, for bathing was her passion. The marsh grasses and reeds grew much taller than she was, so that every so often she reared herself up on her hind legs to see where she was going. She dropped down again to steer a more exact course, each time resuming movement with greater eagerness. As they neared the river, Tilly could smell it. Her pace quickened so that she took the last few yards at a low run, whining. She would never jump in, but entered the water still at a run, and only began swimming when she felt her body beginning to sink.

Tilly swam round and round, whining, while Ben undressed by a willow-tree. He did not bother to put on bathing-trunks, for there was never anyone about. He dived in and swam, and Tilly threshed the water round him.

There was never anyone about – until the last day of Ben's visit. That day, the weather was stiflingly hot, and Ben and Young Tilly bathed in the morning to keep cool. Afterwards, they lay under the willow-tree where, even in its shade, the heat dried fur and skin. They shared the lunch between them – hard-boiled eggs and thick cheese sandwiches, and a bottle of lemonade as an extra for Ben. That made the day seem even heavier and drowsier. They slept.

So not even Tilly was awake when the canoe appeared for the first time, coming out from under the driftway bridge. There were two boys and a little girl in it. Between the knees of the older, red-haired boy, who sat in the stern, was a dog: an upstanding-looking mongrel, mostly terrier perhaps. He glanced towards the bank where Ben and Tilly lay, but they were hidden by the grasses, asleep. No wind blew a scent from them. The canoe passed and went out of sight.

The boy and the dog slept on. Breezes began to blow the leaves of the willow-tree, so that their silvery-green undersides showed light against a darkened sky. Great black clouds crept overhead. Except for the abrupt, shivering little breezes, the air was hot, still, heavy before the storm. Then a single raindrop splashed on Ben's bare shoulder. He woke, and his movement woke Tilly.

The oncoming storm tried its strength out with a few more big drops, and Ben began hurriedly to collect his clothes to dress. Tilly was shivering and whining round him, getting in his way. Then she fell silent, turning towards the river, alert. Ben looked where she was looking, and at once dropped down behind the screen of grasses. The canoe they had missed before was coming back. Seeing the dog in it, Ben put his fingers through Tilly's collar. She had stiffened, but was willing to remain still and quiet.

The canoe was hurrying to get home before the rain. The two boys were paddling with all their might, and – to leave the stern-man quite free – the dog had been sent forward into the bows. There he sat, in front of the little girl, looking ahead over the water and from side to side at the banks. This time, on one of his side glances, the dog saw or smelt Till. There was no doubt of it, and Ben felt Tilly, under his hand, quiver responsively. The dog stood up now to look better at the bank, and the boat rocked as he moved.

'What is it, Toby?' called the boy at the stern; and, from the way he spoke, Ben knew he must be the master of the dog. With a pang he knew it: the boy was not much older than he, he did not look much richer – even the canoe was old and shabby – but he lived in the country, where you could exercise a dog. So he had a dog.

The other boy in the canoe cried that they must not stop for anything Toby had seen on the bank – it was already beginning to rain quite heavily. The canoe sped on. As it went, the dog in the bows turned sideways and finally right round in order to continue looking at the place on the bank where Tilly was. Then the canoe disappeared under the bridge; and the rain was really coming down.

Then Tilly seemed to go mad. She raced up and down the bank, barking, and then flounced into the water, and swam round furiously, barking and snapping at the raindrops as though they were a new kind of fly. Ben had not meant to bathe again, but now, seeing Till in the poppling water, he could not resist. He dived in and swam under her, which always agitated her. He came up in a shallow, and stood with the raindrops fountaining in the water round him and beating on his head and shoulders and rushing down them. 'Tilly! Tilly!' he shouted, for Tilly – now that the canoe had gone far off – was setting off in its pursuit, still barking. She heard Ben and turned, coming back with the same speed as in her going, and with such an impact on Ben's legs when she reached him that they both went down together into the water, their barking and shouting almost drowned in the rushing of water and wind.

Thunder was rolling up, with lightning. They went ashore. Ben pulled on his clothes, and they began to run home. The marshland was becoming a slough; the driftway was becoming a marsh. Black clouds darkened their muddy way; lightning lit it. By the time they reached the refuge of their home-porch, water seemed to be descending from the sky in continuous volume instead of in separate raindrops.

Ben stumbled in through the front door. A pathway of newspapers had been laid from its threshold to the scullery. 'Straight through to a hot bath,' called Mrs Fitch; 'and that dog's too wet and muddy for a decent home.'

'She's not; and she's frightened of lightning,' said Ben. The violence of the storm excused contradiction. He picked up Tilly and carried her along the paper-way into the scullery, his grandmother no longer protesting. In the scullery Grandpa was pouring cans of hot water into a tin bath. He winked when he saw Young Tilly, and fetched a clean sack to rub her down.

Ben had his hot bath, and towelled himself, and Grandpa gave him his dry change of clothes. The rain was streaming in wide rivers down the scullery window. 'We bathed in it, Grandpa,' said Ben, 'as we were going to be caught in it, anyway.' He remembered the hurrying canoe, and described it and its occupants.

'The red-headed one'll be young Codling,' said Grandpa, 'and the others must be Bob Moss's two youngest.'

'And the dog? Does he belong to the red-haired boy?'

'Aye.'

'Tilly was frightened of him.'

'Of young Codling?'

'No, of his dog.'

'She's a sly one,' said Grandpa emphatically, closing one eye. 'That Toby fathered her puppies some two years back. But she's too old for such tricks now.'

Ben sighed. Young Tilly's mother, Old Tilly, had been old when she had had her last litter of puppies, of which Young Tilly had been one; but Young Tilly was now even older than Old Tilly had been then.

The storm continued, and during tea there was a particularly violent outburst. Young Mrs Perkins, sheltering under a raincoat, dashed in from next door to ask, 'You all right?' She said excitedly that this was the worst storm her husband could remember. Granny was saying that the importance of that remark depended upon how far back a person could remember, and that depended upon his age, which might be nothing to speak of. But Mrs Perkins was already dashing home again.

Up to now, Tilly had been hiding under the furniture; now she made a rush to get out through the door after Mrs Perkins. On the very threshold she darted back from a flash of lightning that, branched like a tree, seemed to hang in the sky, ghastly, for seconds. She yelped and fled back again to the shelter of Grandpa's chair. She squeezed under it so far that she stuck, and the old man had to get up to release her.

'Fat, and a coward,' said Granny.

Everyone knew that Tilly was – well, timid, yet she wanted to go out, even in this thunderstorm. She spent all that evening crawling towards the front door, and then dashing back in terror. For the storm continued with lightning, thunder, and floods of rain.

CHAPTER 6

Promises and Rainbows

'This is the weather for Genesis,' Granny had said at last. 'Try chapter six.'

So Ben began to read aloud the Bible story of the great Deluge of rain, the Flood, and Noah and his Ark. For, though afternoon had passed into evening, the wind still rushed at the driftway cottages, the thunder rolled, the lightning flashed, the rain fell in torrents.

Some years ago, when Mrs Fitch had still been active enough to walk to Little Barley chapel on a Sunday, she used to read daily Bible-passages according to the chapel's printed scheme of Scripture-readings. Then arthritis stopped her attending chapel, and – away from it – she threw over the printed scheme and set Grandpa to read the Bible aloud to her from beginning to end, starting him again at the beginning as soon as he came to the end. But, at each time through, Granny became a little more choosy. The Gospels she always heard in their entirety; but the Epistles of Saint Paul were made shorter and shorter each time Grandpa reached them. Granny liked most of the stories of the Old Testament, but occasionally showed impatience with the leading Character: 'That Jehovah – that Jahwa – that Jah!' she said. 'Could have done with a bit more Christian charity sometimes!'

On the evening of the storm, Grandpa handed over to Ben in the midst of the Psalms.

'"Judge me, O Lord,"' read Ben; '"for I have walked in mine integrity –"'

Granny sniffed. 'These goody-goodies! Try him a bit farther on, Ben.'

'"I have not sat with vain persons,"' read Ben. '"neither will I go with dissemblers. I have hated the congregation of evil doers; and will not sit with the wicked –"'

Mrs Fitch said, 'What a very lucky man! Most of us have to sit where we can, and be thankful to get a seat at all, and put up with it without grumbling.'

Ben found himself thinking of the squash on the Yellow Salden bus. He considered, and then said that perhaps the Psalmist hadn't meant –

'Don't say it!' Granny interrupted. 'That's what they used to say at chapel. If there was something that seemed foolish or downright wicked in a Bible reading, they'd say, "Oh, but of course, Sister Fitch, it doesn't really mean that at all." But if it was something that they fancied anyway, they'd say, "Why, but of course, Sister Fitch, it means just what it says." I know 'em!'

Grandpa opened his mouth to defend the chapel, but shut it again. Ben said, 'Shall I go on?'

'No' – for Granny was ruffled; and then she had said, 'This is the weather for Genesis, anyway. Try chapter six.'

Grandpa composed himself with relief to this change; but Granny was still on the alert as Ben read.

'Wait a minute, Ben! How old did you say?'

Ben repeated: '"And Noah was six hundred years old when the flood of waters was upon the earth."'

'Six hundred years old – well, I never!' Granny said ironically. 'But go on, Ben.'

'"And Noah went in, and his sons, and his wife, and his sons' wives with him, into the ark, because of the waters of the flood. Of clean beasts, and of beasts that are not clean –"'

'I see you, Young Tilly!' Granny said suddenly. 'Creeping over the lino again on your filthy paws!' A storm-gust shook the house, and at that – rather than at old Mrs Fitch's words – Tilly fled back to shelter again. 'Go on, Ben.'

'"Of clean beasts, and of beasts that are not clean, and of fowls –"'

'Joe, are you sure you shut all the chicks in?'

'Aye.'

'Go on, Ben.'

'"– of fowls, and of everything that creepeth upon the earth, there went in two and two unto Noah into the ark, the male and the female, as God had commanded Noah. And it came to pass after seven days, that the waters of the flood were upon the earth. In the six hundredth year of Noah's life –"'

Granny said something under her breath which sounded surprisingly like 'Sez you!'

'"– in the second month, the seventeenth day of the month, the same day were all the fountains of the great deep broken up, and the windows of heaven were opened –"'

'Joe!' cried Mrs Fitch. 'The skylight window – you forgot it!'

'No,' said Grandpa. 'I remembered.'

Ben went on with the story to the very end, to the rainbow that God set in the sky after the Deluge: '"I do set my bow in the cloud, and it shall be for a token of a covenant between me and the earth. And it shall come to pass, when I bring a cloud over the earth, that the bow shall be seen in the cloud: and I will remember my covenant, which is between me and you and every living creature of all flesh; and the waters shall no more become a flood to destroy all flesh."'

'"Every living creature of all flesh,"' Granny repeated. 'That's to say, all beasts clean and –' She looked thoughtfully at Tilly, '– unclean.'

'She's not an *unclean* beast,' said Ben; 'she just gets dirty sometimes. So do I.'

'You don't have mud hanging from the ends of your ears, regularly,' Granny said. She mused. 'Fancy taking all that trouble over them: unclean beasts, useless beasts, beasts that eat up the bones for good soup . . .' She marvelled, without irreverence, at God's infinite mercy to those two, dog and bitch, who had boarded the Ark so that, long afterwards, there might be Tilly and Toby and all other dogs on the earth today. So her mind came into the present. 'And you really expected one of those on your birthday, Ben?'

'It was only – only that I thought Grandpa had promised . . .'

Ben's voice died away. Grandpa was looking at the floor between his feet; Granny was looking at Ben. She said: 'And a promise is a promise, as a covenant is a covenant: both to be kept. But, if you're not God Almighty, there's times when a promise can't be kept.' She looked at Grandpa: 'Times when a promise should never have been made, for that very reason.' Now she was looking neither at Ben nor at Grandpa, as she concluded: 'Even so, a promise that can't be kept should never be wriggled out of. It should never be kept twistily. That was wrong.'

Granny in the wrong: that was where she had put herself. There was an appalled silence.

Ben dared not change the subject of conversation too obviously, but he said at last: 'You know, that woolwork dog that you sent instead of the real one – I meant to ask you something about it.' Perhaps he really had meant to do so, but he had been putting his question off from day to day, and here was the last day of his visit. Now, however, he was glad to go upstairs, get the picture from the suitcase where he had left it, and bring it down to Granny.

He handed it to his grandmother back to front, hoping that she would not find the crack in the glass. He pointed to the inscription on the back. 'I don't know what the foreign words mean, or at least I don't know what the first one means.'

Granny had taken the picture into her hands, but without needing to look at it. 'I remember,' she said. 'Two words. Willy said them and explained them. She paused, and then began, 'Chi –,' as though she were going to say 'chicken'. She paused again, and then said slowly and clearly: 'Chi-ki-tee-toe.'

'Oh,' said Ben. 'I see: Chi-ki-tee-toe – Chiquitito.'

'Chi-wah-wah.'

'Chi-wah-wah – Chihuahua,' Ben repeated. 'Chiqui-tito – Chihuahua.'

'According to Willy,' Granny said, 'Chiquitito is a Spanish word – they speak Spanish in Mexico, where the picture comes from. In Spanish, Chico means small; Chiquito means very small; Chiquitito means very, very small. This is the picture of a dog that was called Chiquitito because it was so very, very small.'

Ben looked at the picture – for only the second time, really, since it had come into his possession; the first time had been on his birthday morning. You could see only one side of the dog, of course: it's nose pointing to the left, its tail to the right; it was done in pinky-brown wool, with a black jet bead for an eye. But this was the representation of what had been a real, flesh-and-blood dog – a dog called Chiquitito. 'Chiquitito,' said Ben, as he might have said 'Tilly', or 'Toby'.

'And Chihuahua is the name of the city in Mexico where the dog lived,' said Granny.

'I know.'

'Name and address,' Grandpa said. 'As you might say: Tilly, Little Barley; or Tilly, the Driftway.'

Granny frowned. 'There's more to it than that. The dog belongs to a breed that only comes from this city of Chihuahua, so the breed is called after the city.'

Now Ben remembered where he had seen the word 'Chihuahua'! Not on any map, but in one of the dog-books in the Public Library. He had been looking for borzois and other big dogs, but now he remembered having noticed something about the other extreme for size – the smallest breed of dog in the world: and the name of the breed had been Chihuahua. So this Chiqui-tito had been a very, very small dog of the smallest breed in the world. No wonder the hand in the picture looked so large: it looked large against a dog so very, very, very small. 'The hand really could be a little girl's,' said Ben.

'That's what Willy thought: the hand of the little girl who owned the dog and embroidered its picture.'

Again Ben felt a pang at the thought of someone his own age, or even younger, who had owned a dog. She had lived in Mexico. He had only the roughest idea of that country as wild and mountainous, with jungly forests and erupting volcanoes. But he was sure that there was plenty of open space there, and that the city of Chihuahua would not be the size of London, or with London's dangerous traffic. So the little girl in Mexico had had a dog, while he had not.

'I wonder what she was like – she and her dog.' For he envied her – the girl of whom all you could say was that she had had a right arm and some kind of white dress with long sleeves and ribbons at the wrist – and a dog called Chiquitito.

'I doubt she's gone long ago,' Granny said. 'And her dog. As Willy's gone . . . People and creatures go, and very often their things live after 'em. But even things must go in their own good time.' She handed the picture back to Ben. 'They get worn out, broken, destroyed altogether.' Ben was glad that she had not noticed the crack in the glass. 'And then what's left?'

There was no answer from Ben or his grandfather, but the melancholy wind round the house seemed to say, 'Nothing . . . nothing . . .'

They went to bed early that night, because Ben was catching the first bus to Castleford station the next morning. He could not get to sleep at first, the wind so lamented, the rain so wept at his bedroom window. Then it seemed as if he had been asleep only a little while when he woke with a start. His grandmother, in her nightgown, was standing by his bed. 'Look through the window!' she said. It was daylight, but very early. There were clouds still in the sky, but shifting and vanishing and the rain had almost stopped. 'Look, and you'll see how He keeps His promise – keeps it twice over!' And Ben saw that the early morning sun, shining on rainclouds and rain, had made a double rainbow.

CHAPTER 7

An End –

T he morning of Ben's going was fine, with the
still – almost exhausted – serenity after a long,
wild storm. Blue sky was reflected in the deep puddles
along the driftway as Ben and old Mr Fitch went to
catch the bus.

They nearly missed it. To begin with, Tilly, who
was supposed to be going with them and who would
have been put on her lead in another moment, left
them. She simply turned up the driftway, towards the
river, as they turned down it, towards the road.
Grandpa and Ben wasted some time shouting after her.
She moved fast, and kept her head and her tail down;

but she would not admit by any hesitation or backward glance that she heard her name being called. She was deaf, because she was off on her own this morning.

They gave Young Tilly up, and went on. And then, just as they reached the road, Grandpa said, 'But did you remember to take Willy's little picture off the mantelpiece this morning?'

Ben had left it there the night before, and now he had forgotten it. He was not sure that he really wanted it, but there was no time to stand working things out in his mind. He turned and ran back to the cottage. He startled his grandmother with a second good-bye, snatched up the picture, and was running back along the driftway as the Yellow Salden bus came in sight.

They caught the bus by the skin of their teeth. Ben was carrying Uncle Willy's picture stuffed in his pocket.

In the station at Castleford, the London train was already in, but with some time to wait before it left. Grandpa would not go before that, so Ben leant out of the carriage window to talk to him. There seemed nothing to talk about in such a short time and at a railway station. They found themselves speaking of subjects they would have preferred to leave alone, and saying things that they had not quite intended.

'Tilly didn't know you were off for good this morning,' said Grandpa. 'She'll look for you later today. She'll miss you.'

'I'll miss her,' Ben said.

'Pity you can't take her to London for a bit.'

'She'd hate London,' said Ben. 'Nowhere for a dog to go, near us. Even the River's too dirty and dangerous to swim in.'

'Ah!' said Grandpa, and looked at the station clock: minutes still to go. 'When you thought we should send you a dog, did you think of the spaniel kind, like her?'

'No,' said Ben. He also looked at the clock. 'As a matter of fact – well, do you know borzois?'

'What! Those tall, thin dogs with long noses and curly hair? *Those?*'

'Only one. Or an Irish wolfhound.'

'A *wolfhound?*'

'Or a mastiff.'

'A –' Grandpa's voice failed him; he looked dazed. 'But they're all such big dogs. And grand, somehow. And – and –' He tried to elaborate his first idea: 'And – well, you've got to admit it: *so big.*'

'I wasn't exactly expecting one like that. I was just thinking of it.'

'You couldn't keep such a *big* dog – not in London,' Grandpa said.

'I couldn't keep even a small dog.'

'Perhaps, now,' Grandpa said, 'a really *small* dog –'

The porters were slamming the doors at last; the train was whistling; the guard had taken his green flag from under his arm.

'Not the smallest,' said Ben; and hoped that his grandfather would accept that as final.

'But surely, boy –'

'Not even the smallest dog of the smallest breed.'

'No?'

'Not even a dog so small – so small –' Ben was frowning, screwing up his eyes, trying to think how he could convince an obstinately hopeful old man. The train was beginning to move. Grandpa was beginning to trot beside it, waiting for Ben to finish his sentence, as though it would be of some help.

'*Not even a dog so small you can only see it with your eyes shut,*' Ben said.

'What?' shouted Grandpa; but it was now too late to talk even in shouts. Ben's absurd remark, the unpremeditated expression of his own despair, went unheard except by Ben himself. The thought, like a letter unposted – unpostable – remained with him.

Ben waved a last good-bye from the window, and then sat down. Something in his pocket knocked against the arm-rest, and he remembered that this must be the picture. He looked up at his suitcase on the rack. It had been difficult enough to get it up there; it would be a nuisance to get it down, just to put the picture inside. Even so, he might have done that, except for the other two people in the compartment: the young man with the illustrated magazines would probably not mind; but there was a much older man reading a sheaf of papers he had brought out of his briefcase. He looked as if he would be against any disturbance, any interruption.

Because he had been thinking of it, Ben quietly took out Uncle Willy's picture and, shielding it with one hand, looked at it. This was the third time he had looked at it.

Still looking at the dog, Chiquitito, he recalled his recent conversation. He could not have the smallest dog of the smallest breed in the world. Not even a dog so small that – if you could imagine such a thing – you could only see it with your eyes shut. No dog.

The feeling of his birthday morning – an absolute misery of disappointed longing – swept over him again. He put the little picture down on the seat beside him, leaned his head back, and closed his eyes, overwhelmed.

He had been staring at the woolwork dog, and now, with his eyes shut, he still saw it, as if it were standing on the carriage-seat opposite. Such visions often appear against shut eyelids, when the open-eyed vision has been particularly intent. Such visions quickly fade; but this did not. The image of the dog remained, exactly as in the picture: a pinky-fawn dog with pointed ears, and pop-eyed.

Only – only, the pinky-fawn was not done in wool, and the eye was not a jet bead. This dog was real. First of all, it just stood. Then it stretched itself – first, its forelegs together; then, each hind leg with a separate stretch and shake. Then the dog turned its head to look at Ben, so that Ben saw its other eye and the whole of the other side of its face, which the picture had never shown. But this was not the picture of a dog; it was a real dog – a particular dog.

'Chiquitito,' Ben said; and the dog cocked its head.

Ben had spoken aloud. At the sound of his own

voice, he opened his eyes in a fright. Where the dog had been standing, the young man sat looking at him in surprise; the elderly businessman was also looking – and frowning. Ben felt himself blush. He forgot everything but the need not to seem odd, not to be noticed, questioned.

He turned to look out of the window. He kept his eyes wide open and blinked as briefly and infrequently as possible. He felt two gazes upon him.

After a while the young man spoke to him, offering to lend him one of his magazines. Ben devoted himself deeply to this, until the train was drawing into London.

Now, of course, Ben had to get his suitcase down. The young man, gathering his own things together, helped him. There was some confusion, and the young man's magazines and several other objects fell to the floor. He picked up all his possessions hurriedly, in order to be ready to leave the train as it slowed up to the platform at Liverpool Street. And Ben, looking through the carriage window, caught sight of his mother on the platform – and there was Frankie, too – and Paul! He began to feel the impatience and excitement of homecoming; his mind suddenly filled with it; other thoughts, even the most important, were pushed into the waiting-rooms of his brain. As the young man sprang to the platform, Ben was at his heels. He heaved his suitcase out, and ran.

The elderly businessman was the last to leave the carriage. He put his papers back into his briefcase in an orderly way, re-furled his umbrella, moved over to the mirror for a glance at his tie, and – crunch! The heel of his shoe had trampled something on the floor that should not have been there, and part of which was glass, from the sound of it. This time the woolwork picture suffered more than a crack to its glass. The whole glass was smashed and ground – with dirt from the floor – into the representation of whatever it had been – you could hardly tell now. The frame, too, was utterly broken.

The man looked down in irritation as well as in dismay. He really could not be held responsible. The picture must have belonged to one of the other two passengers, but they were both lost in the streaming crowds by now. He would make himself late if he concerned himself with the further fate of this – this – well, the thing was only a wreck now, anyway. He was going to leave it; and, because he did not even want to think of it, he pushed the thing a little way under one of the seats with his foot. There, a not quite emptied ice-cream carton dribbled over it, completing the destruction of what had once been a picture.

You could hardly blame the cleaner, who came later to sweep out the carriages, for thinking that this was just a bit of old rubbish, dangerous because of the broken glass. The cleaner put it with all the other rubbish to be burnt; and it was.

So the little woolwork picture had gone at last – in its own good time, as Mrs Fitch would have said. During its existence it had given pleasure to a number of people, which is mainly what things are for. It had been lovingly worked by the little girl who lived in the city of Chihuahua and who owned the Chihuahua called Chiquitito. Willy Fitch had found it in a curio shop in a Mexican port – and how it got there from so far inland remains a mystery – and it had pleased him, so that he bought it to take back to his mother as a present. The gift had pleased Mrs Fitch, partly because it came from her son, no doubt; and, much later, she had given it to her grandson. It was true that to Ben himself the woolwork picture had brought bitter disappointment. Now the possibility of its ever having an effect of any kind upon any human being again seemed gone. For the picture itself was gone – broken and utterly destroyed.

As old Mrs Fitch would have said, What's left? It seemed, nothing.

CHAPTER 8

– and a Beginning

*B*en did not go straight home from Liverpool Street Station. This was the last day of the boys' summer holidays, when Mrs Blewitt always gave them a treat. That was why she had brought Frankie and Paul to meet Ben. They all went straight to have baked beans on toast in the station Help-Yourself that overlooks the comings and goings of the trains. There they discussed what they should do with their afternoon. They all – including Ben – suggested and argued; but it was Paul's turn to decide, and he chose the Tower of London – partly because of the ravens.

Ben enjoyed the Tower without foreboding. He said

to himself, 'And I'll have time to think afterwards . . .'

After the Tower, Mrs Blewitt took them to a tea-shop, because she said she had to wash that dank old air out of her throat and voice at once. Then, talking, they went home; and there was Charlie Forrester helping May to fry sausages, and they were both very excited because Charlie really thought he'd found somewhere for them to live when they were married. Charlie worked for a building firm that specialized in the conversion of old houses into flats, and his firm had got him the offer of a flat in a house they were beginning to work on in North London. Cheap, too, for the size – it would be a larger flat than they wanted. But if Dilys would really come and share the flat and share the expense – and Dilys was nodding and laughing – and get her new job in North London . . . Mrs Blewitt listened, watching the sausages bursting but not liking to interrupt, and anyway thinking sadly that North London was a long way from South London. But, as Charlie said, the air was good because that part of London was high – 'and within reach of Hampstead Heath, Mrs B.!'

So, above the spitting of the fat in the frying-pan, Charlie and May and Dilys were telling about the flat in North London, and Frankie and Paul were telling about the Tower, and Ben was just thinking he'd take his suitcase upstairs to unpack quietly, by himself, in the bedroom, when – he remembered. He hadn't put it into the suitcase, after all. He hadn't – he touched his pocket, but knew he hadn't – put it back into his pocket. He must have left the little picture in the railway compartment.

He set down his case and made for the door. But he met his father coming in from work: 'Here! You're not going out, Ben, just when we're all ready to sit down to a hot meal!' And his mother heard, and made him come back. And his father wanted to hear all about his stay with his grandparents, as well as about the flat Charlie had found, and about the Tower of London.

He did not tell them why he had been going out. Secretly he determined to go back to Liverpool Street Station the next day, after school. This evening it would probably have been no use, anyway – too early for lost property to have been brought in. But he would go tomorrow to get the picture back; he must have it. He must.

He had lost the picture, and so he was afraid that he had somehow lost a dog – a dog that answered to the name of Chiquitito.

That evening, as usual, Frankie went to bed first. Then Paul, ten minutes later – just so long because he was older; but no longer, because the two of them always had things to talk about. But the excitement of the day had tired them, and they were both asleep by the time Ben came. He undressed slowly and unhappily, thinking of his loss. He turned off the light and got into bed, but then lay, unhopeful of sleep, with his hands behind his head, staring at the ceiling-shadows cast by the street-lamps outside.

But Ben, too, was tired with a long, full day, and

wearied out with loss and, above all, the old longing. Even before he was ready to sleep, his eyelids fell over his eyes.

He saw nothing; and then he saw a point – something so small that it had neither length nor breadth. But the point was coming towards him, taking on size as it came. He saw what it must be. 'Chiquitito!' he called softly. The dog was racing towards him, appearing ever larger as it came nearer; and yet, when it reached him, it was still very, very small. He realized how small when he stretched out his hand to it: his hand looked like a giant's against such a tiny dog.

The dog curvetted round him, knowing its name, knowing its master. Then it bounded away, expecting to be followed. So they set off together through strange and wonderfully changing countryside. For by now Ben was really entering sleep and his dreams.

This was the beginning of their companionship.

CHAPTER 9

Wolves Die by Hundreds

*B*en never fully understood the coming of the Chihuahua; and at first he feared the possibility of its
going from him as inexplicably. He did not trust his
own need and the dog's responsive devotion.

He thought that material connexion was necessary —
the connexion of some*thing*.

He went again and again to Liverpool Street Station
to ask for his picture. He was frightened when, on his
third successive visit, they told him with finality that
the picture had still not been brought in: it must be
accounted lost for good. Yet, when he closed his eyes
on the succeeding nights, knowing that he would never

,see the picture again, he still saw his Chihuahua.

He thought that knowledge was necessary to give him power over it. He had worried at first that he did not know exactly what Chihuahuas were like, and liked to do. He began to frequent the Public Library again. He exhausted the resources of the Junior Library and – with the librarian's permission – consulted specialist works in the main Library. Moving from dog-book to dog-book, he was gradually collecting what little information is easily available about the lesser foreign breeds.

The dog Chiquitito was companionably interested in Ben's researches and – on the whole – most responsive to suggestion. 'The Chihuahua is very active, alert, intelligent, and affectionate,' said one book. That very night, the dog's actions became as swift as pinky-fawn lightning; its ears cocked in alertness so constant that their muscles must have ached; and intelligence and affection henceforth marked its conduct to an exceptional degree.

Fawn, it seemed, was only one of the colours in which a Chihuahua might appear. 'Colours are varied: white, biscuit, cream, light and dark fawns, lemon, peach, apricot, sable, blue, chocolate, and black.' Ben, reading the list, was overwhelmed by the richness, and – Non-Fiction was such a quiet part of the Public Library – shut his eyes; and there was Chiquitito in blue fur – a soft, smoky blue that was just believable. With shut eyes Ben watched the blue Chihuahua turn slowly round to show the true blueness of every part except its black collar, black markings, black nose, and bead-black eyes. It seemed to fancy itself.

When at last Ben reopened his eyes, he found the librarian staring at him. Hurriedly he went back to his looking and reading. But the librarian still observed him. She did not like a boy of that age hanging about in the main Library, even if he had special permission and even if he did stick to the Poultry, Dogs, and Bee-keeping shelves. Now he was reading in another book; and now – look; he had gone a greeny-white in the face. The librarian went over to him at once.

'It says they were considered edible,' said Ben. 'What's 'edible'?'

'Eatable,' said the librarian. 'But you feel ill, don't you?'

'I thought it meant that,' said Ben. 'Yes, I do feel rather sick. But I only *feel* sick: I shan't be.'

The librarian, hoping that he was right, made him sit down in a chair, behind which she opened a window. The boy's complexion returned to normal, and he said he would go home. He wanted to take the book out.

The librarian held out her stamp over the date-slip, and then came out with what was in her mind: 'You know, boys of your age should be borrowing books from the Junior Library, not from here.'

'But I told you,' said Ben: 'the books on my subject in the other library are so babyish.'

The librarian looked at the title of the book he wanted to borrow. 'Dogs – there's an excellent book which must be in the Junior Library: *Ten Common Breeds of Dog in Britain and their Care.*'

'I've looked,' said Ben. 'It was no good – truly.'

The librarian stamped *Dogs of the World* for him, but held on to the volume for a moment as she asked, 'And why are you so interested in this subject of yours? Have you a dog of your own, or are you going to get one?'

Ben hesitated, and then said carefully: 'Yes, I have a dog; and no, I'm not going to get one.'

'If you have a dog already,' the librarian pointed out, 'of course you're not going to get one. One dog must be difficult enough to look after properly, in London.'

'It's a small dog,' Ben explained. 'So small that –' He shut his eyes as he spoke, and held them shut for several seconds, so that the librarian wondered if the child were feeling ill again. But then he opened his eyes to finish what he was saying, rather lamely: 'Well, it's *small*.'

The librarian, watching him go out with the book under his arm, still felt uneasy. She was sure there was something wrong somewhere, even if she could not put her finger upon it. She would feel happier, anyway, when he went back to the Junior Library, where he belonged.

That night, in bed, Ben read a little more about the Chihuahua in ancient Mexico. Then he turned out the light, and shut his eyes as usual.

He drifted into sleep, and then into nightmare. Paul and Frankie slept through his screaming, but his mother came. She roused him. Like a much younger child he clung to her, sobbing: 'People with sort of toasting-forks were chasing us, to catch us and cook us and eat us. And they'd fattened us up first.'

Mrs Blewitt tried to soothe Ben by bringing him to a sense of present reality. 'But look, here I am; and here you are, safe in bed; and there are Paul and Frankie, still asleep. No one's chasing us all to eat us.'

'I wasn't with you and Paul and Frankie,' said Ben. 'And they did fatten them to eat them – the book said so.'

'A nightmare about cannibals,' said Mrs Blewitt over her shoulder to Mr Blewitt, who had followed to see what was the matter.

'Not cannibals,' Ben said. 'They used to eat – to eat –' He wanted no one to know his secrets, but his mother was close and he had been so afraid. 'Well, they used to eat Chi – Chi –'

'To eat chickens?'

'No. Chi – Chi –'

'Cheese?'

He told the truth, but not all of it: 'They used to eat – dogs.'

Mr Blewitt said under his breath, 'Dogs!' Mrs Blewitt frowned at him. She made Ben lie down again, gave him an aspirin, and told him not to dream any more.

Back in their own bedroom, Mrs Blewitt said, 'I told you what it must mean, Bill – his bringing home all those library books about dogs. And now this nightmare. He's still hankering to have a dog.'

Mr Blewitt groaned. He sometimes felt that his five children and their affairs were almost too much for him: May's wedding-plans, and Dilys wanting to leave home with her, too, and now Ben's dog ... Mr Blewitt loved his children, of course, but it was really a great relief, nowadays, to go off to work – to slip down the Underground, where there were hundreds of thousands of people on the move, but none of his business so long as they had their tickets and kept clear of the doors. If some of them wanted dogs and could not have them, that was strictly their affair, not his.

'He just can't have a dog in London,' Mr Blewitt said, out of all patience. 'I'll tell him so, now and for the last time.' He was starting back towards the boys' bedroom.

'No, Bill,' said Mrs Blewitt, 'not now; and I'll tell him myself – when there's a right time for it.'

The time did not come the next day, for Ben was at school in the morning and afternoon, and called at the Public Library on the way home; and, when he got home, his mother was just setting out with May and Dilys to meet Charlie Forrester and see the flat.

Ben spent the evening reading his latest book from the Library.

'They are small –', he read of the Chihuahua: well, yes, very, very small, especially some: '– pet dogs –', well, perhaps, although 'pet' sounded rather womanish '– and very timid.' Very *timid*? Ben felt shocked and incredulous. Timid – now, you might call Young Tilly timid – although Grandpa said she was really just prudent; but then, you took Tilly as you found her –

you had to. The dog Chiquitito was different – not subject to imperfection.

Unwillingly he remembered that, the night before, the Chihuahua and he had both fled before the ancient and hungry Mexicans. He admitted that he himself had been terrified; but the Chihuahua – had not its accompanying him been an act of affection – of close loyalty – rather than of timidity? Was his dog really a coward? Only the evidence of his own eyes would convince him of that.

That night, when he closed his eyes, he saw a landscape even before he saw the dog in it. The scene appeared familiar and then he remembered: Russia. The whole landscape was white with snow, except for the dark woods where the wolves hid themselves. There were the sleighs covered with white woollen blankets, and men beating the woods. The wolves came out – they were much larger than Ben had ever imagined them before, huge, with gnashing teeth; and there were dozens of them – one whole pack at least. From the dark, distant woods they came rushing towards the sleighs, and in their very path stood Ben.

Then he realized that the dog Chiquitito stood beside him. This time it was black in colour – Ben had never before seen such an absolute, such a resolute black. The dog looked up at him. Very *timid*? The Chihuahua's pop eyes seemed almost to start from its head in indignation; and at once it set off, with the greatest activity. It raced across the snow to meet the oncoming wolf-packs; it was like a swift moving bead of jet against the snow. It reached the wolf-leader, and the black point rose to the grey mass. There was a dreadful howling, and red blood, and the wolf-leader lay dead, and the black point moved on. The Chihuahua was only a hundredth part of the size of any wolf, and the wolves were at least a hundred times as many; but it opposed them with activity and intelligence and, above all, with incredible daring. The dog was more like David against Goliath, more like Sir Richard Grenville at Flores, than any ordinary Chihuahua against several packs of wolves. Ben watched; the borzoi dogs came out from under their white woollen blankets to watch in amazement and deep respect. When every wolf of every pack lay dead in its own blood on the snowy plain, the dog Chiquitito trotted back. One ear was slightly torn.

Ben said to him, before them all: 'Not in the least timid – never. On the contrary, bold and resolute. Very, very brave.' The huntsmen by the sleighs, who had not even troubled to take out their hunting knives to finish the wolves off, seemed to understand, for they clapped. The dog Chiquitito modestly lowered its eyes and, under Ben's very gaze, its whole body blushed – turned from the original resolute black through a pinky-grey to a deep peach. Then that colour slowly ebbed and muddied until the dog was its usual fawn.

And so, the next day, Ben took the dog-book back to the Public Library and said that he did not want any more books on that subject, anyway. The librarian was relieved.

71

And that evening, when his mother took Ben aside to begin her little talk ('You know, Ben, you had a nightmare because of all this reading about dogs'), Ben said: 'I've given up dog-books, this very day. One of them turned out to be such rubbish.'

'But, all the same,' his mother persisted, 'you're still thinking about a dog.' Ben did not deny this. 'You're still wanting to have a dog.'

'No!' said Ben. 'No, truly! I'm not wanting a dog any more, because I've *got* –'

'Yes?'

Ben changed his mind about what he was going to say. 'I've got over it.'

CHAPTER 10

London Exploits

Mrs Blewitt could hardly believe that Ben no longer wanted a dog. In her experience, he did not give ideas up easily; besides, if he were like Paul or Frankie, he needed an animal of some kind. Well, within reason, he could have any small one that wasn't a dog.

'How would you like a white mouse, like Frankie's?' Mrs Blewitt asked.

'No, thank you. I don't want a white mouse.'

'Well, then –' Mrs Blewitt swallowed hard: 'well, then, a white rat?'

'No, thank you,' said Ben. 'I don't want anything at

all. I just want people to leave me alone. Please.'

He really meant what he said: to be left alone, in peace and quiet, so that he could shut his eyes, and see. For, by now, night-time visions were not enough for him. He saw the dog Chiquitito as soon as he closed his eyes in bed, and they were together when he fell asleep, entering his dreams together. But, when he woke in the morning, a whole day stretched before him, busy and almost unbearably dogless.

You might have thought that week-ends and half-holidays would have provided Ben with his opportunity, but not in a family such as the Blewitts. Ben's mother did not like his staying indoors if the weather were fine; and, if it were wet, too many other people seemed to stay indoors.

So Ben reflected, as he slipped up to his bedroom one wet Saturday afternoon. He had left his father downstairs watching football on television; May and Dilys were cutting out dress patterns; Mrs Blewitt was advising her daughters and making a batch of buns for tea; Paul had disappeared, and Frankie –

When Ben reached the bedroom, there was Frankie. He was sitting cross-legged and straight-backed on his bed: this meant that he was exercising his white mouse. The mouse ran round and round his body, between his vest and his skin, above the tightened belt. In her ignorance of this Mrs Blewitt always marvelled that Frankie's vests soiled so quickly – had such a *trampled* look.

At least there was no Paul in the bedroom, although

Paul's pigeon loitered on the window-sill, peering in.

But Frankie was going to talk. 'I suppose it's because you're older than I am that you can have one ... A white *rat*! And Mother always used to say that the very idea made her feel sick!' Mrs Blewitt's offer to Ben had gradually become known. Such a piece of information seeps through a family to any interested members, rather as water seeps through a porous pot.

'But I don't want a rat.' Ben climbed on to his bed and composed himself as if for a nap.

'If you take the rat,' said Frankie, 'I'll trade for it: some really good marbles –'

'No,' said Ben.

'– and I've a shoe-box full of bus tickets. And another of milk-bottle tops.'

'No.'

'You're a grabber,' Frankie said coldly. 'But, all right, you can have it: my penny flattened on the railway line.'

'No,' said Ben. 'I told you: I'm not having the rat. I don't want it. I just want to be left alone. I just want peace and quiet to shut my eyes.'

There was a very short silence. Then Frankie said, 'This is our room just as much as yours, and I can talk in it as much as I like; and you look just silly lying there with your eyes shut.'

'Go away.'

Frankie went on grumbling about his rights, which distracted Ben. Then he fell abruptly and absolutely silent, which was distracting in a different way. Ben opened his eyes and jerked his head up suddenly. Sure enough, he caught Frankie at it – sticking out his tongue, wriggling his hands behind his ears, all at Ben, in the most insulting manner.

'I've told you to go away, Frankie.'

'This is our room as well as yours. Some day it'll be only ours, and then you won't be allowed to come in at all without our permission.' This was a reference to the re-allotting of bedrooms that would follow May's marriage and Dilys's leaving home with her. The girls' bedroom would be left empty. Ben, as the eldest of the remaining children, was to move into it, by himself. He looked forward to the time: then at least he would be allowed to shut his eyes when he wanted.

'And until then we just kindly let you share this room with us,' said Frankie.

'Go away, I say!'

'A third part of it, exactly – to look silly in, with your eyes shut!'

Frankie was goading Ben; Ben was becoming en-raged. It was all more unbearable than Frankie knew. Ben was not allowed even a dog so small that you could only see it with your eyes shut, because he was not allowed to shut his eyes.

At least he was bigger and stronger than Frankie. He became tyrannical. 'Get off that bed and go away – now!'

Frankie said, 'You're just a big bully.' But he *was* smaller and weaker, and he had the responsibility of the white mouse. He got off the bed – carefully, because of the mouse – and went away.

Ben felt only depressed by his unpleasant triumph. He was at last alone, however. He shut his eyes: the dog Chiquitito sat at the end of the bed . . .

Suddenly Ben was sure in his bones that he was still being watched. He opened his eyes a slit. There seemed no one. The pigeon was staring through the glass – but not at him. Ben opened his eyes altogether to follow the direction of the bird's gaze: below Paul's bed lay Paul. He had been going through his stamp–album, but now he was watching Ben with curiosity.

'Spying on me!' Ben shouted with violence.

Paul rolled out of reach of his clawing hand, and said: 'I wasn't! There was nothing to spy on, anyway. You were just lying there with your eyes shut and a funny look on your face.' But he scrambled out of reach of Ben's fury, and fled. Ben locked the bedroom door after him, although he knew that he had not the least right to do such a thing. He shooed the pigeon off the window-sill. Then, with a sigh, he composed himself upon the bed once more to shut his eyes and see the dog Chiquitito in real peace . . .

Almost at once Paul came back, having fetched Frankie. They rattled the doorknob and then chanted alternating strophes of abuse through the keyhole. Frankie ended by shouting, 'You're not fit to have a white mouse, let alone a white rat!' Their father came upstairs to see what the noise was, and made Ben unlock the door. Then his mother called them all for tea. That was that.

So, as Ben was clearly never going to see enough of

his dog in the privacy of his own home, he began to seeks its companionship outside. He discovered the true privacy of being in a crowd of strangers.

In a Tube train, for instance, Ben could sit with his eyes shut for the whole journey, and if anyone noticed, no one commented. He felt especially safe if he could allow himself to be caught by the rush-hour, and on the Inner Circle Tube. The other passengers, sitting or strap-hanging or simply wedged upright by the pressure of the crowd, endured their journey with their eyes shut – you see them so, travelling home at the end of any working-day in London. Like them, Ben kept his eyes shut, but he was not tired. And when the others got out at their various stations, he stayed on, going round and round on the Inner Circle – it was fortunate that Mr Blewitt never knew of it – and always with his eyes shut. No one ever saw what he was seeing: a fawn-coloured dog of incredible minuteness.

If Ben were sitting, he saw the dog on his knee. If he stood, he looked down with his shut eyes and saw it at his feet. The dog was always with him, only dashing ahead or lingering behind in order to play tricks of agility and daring. When Ben finally left the Tube train, for instance, the Chihuahua would play that dangerous game of being last through the closing doors. While Ben rode up the Up escalator with his eyes shut, the Chihuahua chose to run up the Down one, and always arrived at the top first. Only a Chihuahua called Chiquitito could have achieved that – and in defiance of the regulation that wisely says that dogs must be carried on escalators. This dog exulted before its master in deeds which would have been foolhardy – in the end, disastrous – for any other creature. On all these occasions the dog's coat was black, as it had been for the encounter with the thousand wolves.

On buses, the Chihuahua sprang on or off when the vehicle was moving, as a matter of course. (Ben trembled, even while he marvelled.) But its greatest pleasure was when Ben secured the front seat on the top deck, and they went swaying over London together. Ben had always loved that; and all the things that Ben liked doing in London, the dog Chiquitito liked too.

Ben would walk to the bridge over the River, rest his elbows on the parapet, and shut his eyes. There was the dog Chiquitito poised on the parapet beside him. The parapet was far enough above the water to have alarmed a dog such as Tilly, but not this much smaller dog. Without hesitation, it would launch itself into the void, and, in falling, its tininess became even tinier, until it reached the water, submerged, and came up again, to sport in the water round unseeing crews and passengers on river-craft.

Then Ben whistled softly and briefly. At once the swimmer turned to the bank with arrow-swiftness, reached a jetty, leaped up the steps, ran under a locked gate (any other dog would have had at least to squeeze through), and disappeared from view. A moment later the dog trotted back on to the bridge, to where Ben waited.

Once Ben used to wonder what a Mexican Chihuahua thought of the greasy, filthy London Thames after the wild, free rivers of its native country. But nothing of the smell, dirt, noise, traffic, and other roaring dangers of London daunted the Chihuahua. It seemed to take London for granted. It never even cocked an ear when Big Ben boomed the hour.

One day Ben noticed a small silver plate on the dog's collar: an address-plate. Here he read the name of the dog and the name of its home city, as on the back of the lost picture. But the name of the home city had changed:

CHIQUITITO

LONDON

CHAPTER 11

A Christmas Eve to Remember

*B*en Blewitt was just an ordinary boy with an unsurprising character and abilities – except for his ability to see a dog too small to be there. Unlike the Chihuahua, he had never been a daredevil; he was inclined to be rather slow and cautious. Perhaps for that very reason he took a particular delight in the dog's feats.

And still he had to have more and more of his dog's company. In school, now, he would often sit with a studious-seeming hand shielding his shut eyes, watching the dog Chiquitito as it leapt from desk-top to desk-top in a kind of wild, impertinent sport.

He heard only absent-mindedly the voices of the other pupils and of the master. His attention was entirely upon his Chihuahua. Look! the creature was almost flying through the air now, in its daredevil leaps – and under the teacher's very nose, too!

'What have I been saying, Blewitt?'

Ben opened his eyes, and did not know. He never knew the answers to questions in class nowadays. Angry schoolmasters reprimanded him and punished him for inattention. Still he persisted in watching his Chihuahua whenever he could. He had never been a brilliant boy in school; now he seemed a stupid one. He knew it, without being able to care. He supposed that his termly report would not be a good one, perhaps not even passable. His father would be severe; his mother would grieve. Still he must watch his Chihuahua.

'Blewitt – Blewitt, I say! Open your eyes – or is there something wrong with them?' And by now the question was not sarcastic. Word went privately from the form master right up to the Head, and then went privately right down again to Mrs Blewitt, who was asked to call upon the headmaster one afternoon. The Head said that he did not wish to worry Mrs Blewitt unduly. Her son's odd behaviour recently might be due to no more than faulty eyesight, possibly to be corrected by the wearing of glasses. The Head's suggestion of an immediate and thorough testing of the boy's eyes, merely as a precaution, should not alarm Mrs Blewitt.

At once Mrs Blewitt was alarmed, and more than alarmed. She felt some foreboding that no oculist could dispel; but she took Ben to have his eyes tested.

The oculist's conclusion was that Ben had excellent eyesight; he could read even the tiniest test-lettering. Outside again, Ben said to his mother, 'I told you that I could see even the smallest things. As a matter of fact, I know I can see things so small that other people can't see them at all. There's nothing wrong with my eyes.'

'Then why do you sit with them shut so often? I've caught you at it at home; they say you do it at school. You're not short of sleep.'

'My eyes are tired.'

'The oculist is positive that they're not.'

'They're not tired *by* seeing things,' Ben said carefully. 'They're tired *of* seeing things – the same old things – great hulking things, far too big – big, dull, ordinary things that just behave in the same dull old way –'

'If you mean your teachers and the other boys, you are speaking very rudely indeed!'

Ben sighed. 'I didn't mean to. I was really thinking of what my eyes would rather see, that's all.'

'But, Ben dear, just tell me *why* –'

'I've told you.'

It was Mrs Blewitt's turn to sigh. She gave up; but from now on, secretly and fearfully, she watched Ben.

The dog Chiquitito was becoming a continuous presence for Ben. When the boy's eyes were shut, the dog was there, visibly; and when his eyes were open, the dog still seemed present – invisibly. Ben felt it there – knew it was there, now loyally and alertly beside him, now with its active and bold spirit speeding it to engage in some new and extraordinary exploit. Always the dog was either before Ben's eyes or in his mind. His mother, watching him when he did not know he was being watched, saw him with eyes open but vacant – abstracted and absorbed, she supposed, in some inward vision. She told herself that the boy slept well, ate well, and admitted to no worries; but she was uneasy.

Meanwhile, autumn was settling into winter, with fog.

In the country, the fog was white. Old Mr and Mrs Fitch watched it rise from the ploughed fields round the house and thicken from the direction of the river. Grandpa watched the solid Tilly fade and vanish into it, when she slipped off on one of her private expeditions down the driftway; and she would come back with the hairs of her coat beaded with moisture. Grandpa himself went out as little as he could; but the damp seemed to seep indoors to find him, so that he began to complain of aches in the back. Old Mrs Fitch said that his back must be ironed with a hottish iron over brown-paper. She could not do it herself, nowadays, but Mrs Perkins came in from next door and – under Mrs Fitch's direction – gave him this relief.

Then the two of them settled by the fire again, and Tilly was allowed to lie on the rug between them, where she groaned and twitched in her sleep, dreaming of summer and of other dogs, no doubt. And the soft whiteness of the fog drifted up to the window, pressed against the glass, and looked in on them.

In London, the fog that came up from the River was whitish, too; but later, another fog began. No one could say where it was coming from, but everyone could taste its tang in the air, and feel the oppression of its descent. The sky seemed to thicken, and at the same time to come lower – so low and heavy, it looked as if it would soon need propping up with poles. And then, at last, one day when all indoor lights were on by three o'clock in the afternoon, the sky fell and lay upon London in a greasy, grey-yellow pea-souper of a London fog.

People were saying that soon you really might as well walk in London with your eyes shut. Ben tried it, going slowly, of course, along the pavements of streets he knew well. The Chihuahua, now lemon-yellow in colour – perhaps for better visibility – went slightly ahead. It seemed to know the streets as well as Ben did, going not too fast, but with an unerring sense of direction. Ben followed with absolute trust; he gave himself into the Chihuahua's care.

All landmarks and familiarities melted into fog. Pedestrians fumbling their way home overtook even-slower-moving vehicles; as the fog thickened, they would come up abruptly against cars abandoned half on the pavement. By that time, the buses, having reached the safety of their garages, refused to venture out again.

The streets filled with fog and emptied of traffic and people. Nobody in London went out unless he had to – except for Ben. In the evening he slipped from the house to roam the streets with the dog Chiquitito. Fog enclosed them in a world of their own. They owned it, and they owned each other. For, if Ben were the Chihuahua's master, the dog itself possessed Ben's eyes and thoughts, directed his actions.

At last the fog cleared away into sparkling cold weather in time for the very beginning of the Christmas rush. The Blewitts began to get ready for their Christmas. May was knitting hard to finish a pullover for Charlie; Mrs Blewitt was gathering things for a Christmas hamper to go to Granny and Grandpa; Christmas cards and parcels had to be posted early to Mrs Blewitt's brother in Canada; and soon all the Blewitts were busy making or buying presents for aunts, uncles, cousins, and for each other.

All except for Ben. Usually, at Christmas, he would join with May and Dilys or with Paul and Frankie in giving presents. This year, May and Dilys thought he must be joining with Paul and Frankie; and Paul and Frankie thought he must be joining with May and Dilys. He was doing neither, nor was he preparing to give presents on his own. Ben had regretted the passing of the fog, and he simply could not be bothered with the coming of Christmas. He cared for another thing.

This year, Mr Blewitt said, their family Christmas must be rather quieter than usual – certainly less expensive – because of May's wedding so soon afterwards. Plans for the wedding were already mixing with preparations for Christmas. May had come out into the open with her ambition for a page-boy at her wedding.

There was a terrible scene when Frankie, who had been making multicoloured paper-chains and paying no attention, realized that they wanted *him*. Paul, knowing that he himself was too large for the part, laughed so much that he fell over on to the heap of paper-chains, to Frankie's double fury. Dilys stood by May; Mr Blewitt stood by Frankie. Mrs Blewitt seemed to waver between the two sides but finally came down on Frankie's by reminding them all of a little cousin who might act in Frankie's place. The boy was only five, hardly old enough to object or even to realize into what he was being led, and Mrs Blewitt was sure his mother would agree. She fetched a recent photograph of the child. May and Dilys said that he looked sweet; Mr Blewitt said that with those curls he would be useful as either page or bridesmaid. Paul stopped laughing at Frankie, and they both went back to the paper-chains.

To all this Ben was as if deaf and blind; none of it – Christmas or wedding – concerned him.

This was the last Christmas for the Blewitts as just one family – before May Blewitt became Mrs Charlie Forrester. So Mr Blewitt had decided on a special family treat: he would take everyone up to the West End to see the decorations and lights and the shops and to have tea. He would take them on Christmas Eve itself – he had that day off instead of Boxing Day.

This was just the kind of interruption to his thoughts and visions that fretted and wearied Ben. He did not want to go with the others, and he said so to his mother. But Mrs Blewitt was determined that her husband should have the pleasure of seeing the whole family enjoying his treat. Ben was not ill; he had nothing else to do (no one knew of those unbought, unmade Christmas presents); he *must* come; he *must* enjoy himself.

The West End on the afternoon of Christmas Eve was as Ben had known it would be: people – people – people; and lights – chains of twinklers and illuminations of fantastic design slung to and fro across the main streets. And people – people – people; and shop-windows in which objects glittered frostily or shone with coloured lights or turned and turned for the ceaseless attraction of the passing people – people – people. So many people pressing and passing that Ben lost his sense of a Chihuahua with him; and yet he never dared to close his eyes to look for it, since so many people were always telling him to keep them particularly wide open. As he blundered unwillingly along, strangers said, 'Look where you're going, sonny!' and his father said, 'Look sharp and keep with us, boy!'; and the rest of the family told each other and him, over and over again, 'Look!', or 'Just look there!', or 'You must just look at that!'

When at last they queued up for their tea, Ben hoped to be able to take a quick glance at his Chihuahua; but he found his mother looking at him, and he dared not shut his eyes. When they sat down to tea, she was opposite to him, and he felt her eyes still upon him with a subdued anxiety. He must wait for some later opportunity.

On the bus on the way home the whole Blewitt family secured the two seats just inside the door, facing each other. They sat three a side, with Frankie on his father's knee, and laughed and talked across the gangway. Only Ben sat silent, and Mrs Blewitt watched him, and he knew that she watched him. His eyes ached with the effort of keeping open when they wanted to shut – to *see*. He was tormented by the longing to see his dog, that must be on the bus with him at this minute. Surely it was. As the bus passed Big Ben and then over the bridge, the dog must recognize a favourite scene. While Mr Blewitt was still ringing the bell for their Request Stop, the dog – with all the daring of a Chihuahua – would be leaping off the platform of the moving bus. Now it must be waiting for them on the pavement. Now it must be trotting ahead of them as the family began to walk the rest of their way home. Now it must have stopped for them to catch up at the traffic-lights, where they had to cross the road.

The lights were changing to green, and the traffic was beginning to move forward. The Blewitts, knowing that they must wait, bunched together, talking again of the afternoon. 'Mother!' said Frankie. 'Did you see the toy fire-engine – but did you see it? Did you?' He pulled impatiently at her sleeve, because she was looking over his head, watching Ben.

Ben stood a little apart from the rest of his family, with his back to them. He was facing squarely on to the road, so that only passing drivers might see that at last he was closing his eyes.

He was sure that the Chihuahua was at his feet. He turned his shut eyes downwards and – with overwhelming joy and relief – saw it. The dog's colour was black. The intrepid creature looked up at him for an instant, then sprang forward to cross the road among the streaming traffic; and Ben followed it.

A moment can last – or seem to last – a long time; and two moments must last twice as long. For the first moment Ben was simply following his dog Chiquitito. The roar of the moving traffic – broken now by the sharper sound of brakes – was nothing to him. Only, there was a woman's voice screaming his name, 'Ben!' It was his mother's calling him back – oh! but it was surely too late – to safety. The syllable of her scream pierced to Ben's tranced mind and heart. It opened his eyes.

In the second moment he thought that, with open eyes – eyes that see the things that all eyes see – he actually saw the dog Chiquitito. He saw the Chiquitito that had been his companion now for so many weeks; he also saw the Chiquitito that had been worked in wool long ago by the nameless little girl in the white dress; and he also saw no dog – that is, the no-dog into which the other two vanished like one flame blown out, into nothingness. And the last dog he was master of: no-dog. He had no dog.

In that same, second moment, a car with screeching brakes hit Ben a glancing blow that flung him forward towards a van whose driver was also stamping on his brake and wrenching at his wheel. As the vehicles came to a standstill, Ben fell to the road between them.

The boy lay unconscious, bleeding, one leg unnaturally twisted. Mrs Blewitt was not allowed to take him into her arms, as she tried to do, lest he had some internal injury which movement might make worse. A policeman came. An ambulance came. The men very carefully loaded Ben Blewitt on to their stretcher and put him inside. His parents went with him to the hospital.

The other Blewitts went home under May's care. Frankie and Paul were sobbing, and Dilys comforted them, but she was crying too. They left the crowd of spectators staring at Ben's blood on the road, and a policeman taking down names and addresses and other information from drivers and other witnesses. The driver of the car that had hit Ben was a grey-haired woman. She could not answer the policeman's questions for crying into her handkerchief and repeating over and over again: 'But he walked straight into the road with his eyes shut – *with his eyes shut!*'

And the van driver supported her evidence. 'He was walking like a sleepwalker – or like a blind man – a blind man being led – you know, a blind man following a guide-dog.'

CHAPTER 12

Mr Fitch Spells Aloud

*B*en had a broken leg, three broken ribs, a broken collarbone, and concussion. The hospital thought that there were no internal injuries; the bones should mend well, especially at Ben's age; but the concussion was severe.

He was a long time recovering consciousness. During that time his mind wandered in a kind of no-man's-land between waking and dreaming. Through this land he went in search of his dog. All the places he had ever known or read of or heard of or even dreamed of mixed together, and mixed with the dog he sought. At one time he was with Young Tilly on the driftway bridge over the River Say, and she would not dive even from that little height into the river because she was afraid. She ran away, howling, and there was a shadow over the bridge. Ben thought it was cast by a storm-cloud, until, looking up, he saw a Mexican volcano that he had never noticed before, towering up at the other end of the driftway. Tilly had gone, but there were three other dogs, and he seemed to hear Granny Fitch's voice saying, 'A promise kept three times over!' For the three dogs were all his. One was the dog embroidered in wool by the little girl with the ribboned white sleeve: Ben could see that – strictly as in the picture – the dog had only one side to its wool-work body and only one eye, of a black bead. The second dog was the dog so small that you could only see it with your eyes shut, and it was black. The third was no-dog.

Then, always, something terrible began to happen. The volcano would begin to erupt; and, instead of running away from it, the dogs – led by the coal-black Chihuahua – ran towards it, and Ben ran after them. He gained on them – he almost had them. But then the first two dogs vanished, leaving only no-dog: Ben had no dog. He began to scream, and when he listened to his voice he recognized his mother's, screaming 'Ben!', as she called him back to safety.

Or perhaps the three dogs led him towards fierce hungry men with toasting-forks and, of the three dogs, all vanished but no-dog: Ben had no dog. Then he began to scream, and it was his mother screaming and calling him back: 'Ben!'

Or perhaps the three dogs sped across a snowy plain towards a thousand packs of wolves, and suddenly two dogs vanished, leaving no-dog: Ben had no dog. And the calling back began again, 'Ben!'

Over and over again the woolwork dog vanished and the black-coated Chihuahua vanished and Ben found that he had no dog, and heard his mother calling his name. But gradually the visions and terrors became – not less confused, for they always remained that – but less continuous. They dimmed, too, as firelight does in a room into which sunshine enters.

His mother said 'Ben' instead of calling it. She spoke it quietly and very carefully, as though trying to wake him without startling him. Ben opened his eyes, and there she was, in her hat and coat, sitting by his bed in the hospital. She saw at once that his eyes were open and looking at her, and she put out her fingers to touch his cheek so that he should know that she was quite real, and that he was getting better. Then Ben closed his eyes again for a while.

Christmas Day was over without Ben's ever having known it. The Blewitt family had hardly noticed it at all, anyway, because of his lying unconscious in hospital. Drearily, too, they had decided that May's wedding must be put off, and Charlie Forrester, with May crying on his shoulder, said that he understood and that it was no use people getting married when they felt so miserable.

But then the hospital promised that Ben would fully recover, even if his recovery took some time; and a postponement of the wedding would really be very awkward, for all the guests had been invited and the arrangements made. Granny Fitch, for example, was sending Grandpa up to London – an expedition he had not made for many, many years. And the mother of the curly haired little cousin had already written that he was beginning to ask for his hair to be cut short like other boys' and she did not know how much longer she could manage to keep him looking as a page-boy should. Taking everything into consideration, Mrs Blewitt thought that May should have her wedding at the proper time, even if Ben could not be there and Mr Blewitt muttered that, in some ways, Ben was a lucky boy to be in hospital.

May smiled again, and Charlie looked relieved and Ben, when he was asked, said that he did not mind. So the wedding would take place on the day fixed, after all.

The only difference to Ben was in his being visited. Since he first went into hospital, his mother had never failed to come daily. But now she warned him that the house would be full of guests on May's wedding-day and that she really could not be sure of managing to slip away. She promised that someone else of the family would come in the afternoon, and she would try to come in the evening, if she possibly could.

A day without a visitor at all would have been very dull. There were only two other occupants of Ben's small ward: a boy who had to lie on his back and spoke very little, and a child – a baby, really – who stared silently at Ben through the bars of his cot. There was a window, but from Ben's bed one had a view only of sky. On the day of the wedding the sky was a wintry blue – the New Year had been cold but fine, so far.

The morning passed, and then the early afternoon, and at last Ben's visitor came. Somehow he had not expected Grandpa to be the one. Old Mr Fitch was wearing not only his blue suit but a blue hat as well, in honour of his grand-daughter's wedding. He took his hat off as he sidled into the ward. He managed with difficulty as he was also carrying a bunch of very short-stemmed snowdrops and a large Oxo tin tied with string.

'Well, boy!' Grandpa whispered. He tiptoed up to Ben's bed and put the snowdrops on the bedtable. 'Just a few – the first – from up the driftway. Picked 'em myself early this very morning.' He put the Oxo tin with them and tapped it. 'Six. Your granny says you're to tell the nurses not to mix 'em up with shop ones for the other patients, and they're to boil them a good five minutes, being new laid. You like a runny yolk and hard white.'

Grandpa then sat down on the visitor's chair, put his hat under it, and his hands on his knees, so that he was comfortable. Then he looked round at the boy in the bed, the boy in the cot, and at all the ward.

'What was the wedding like?' Ben asked. Grandpa turned back to him and remembered that Mrs Blewitt had told him to entertain Ben by describing the wedding-party. He went through the guests – Forresters and Blewitts and Fitches. The Fitch relations had outnumbered the other two put together – Bill Blewitt was an orphan with only one sister, anyway. Then Grandpa went on to the food and the drink.

Ben listened languidly. He stared as he listened, wondering at the oddity of his grandfather being here, in the middle of London, instead of in Castleford, or Little Barley, or at the driftway. Sometimes Grandpa paused to look round him, as if similarly surprised, even alarmed. When a nurse came in, he got up in a fright, nearly knocking his chair over, and treading on his hat. She smiled at him, made him sit down again, and began attending to her cot-patient.

To put his grandfather at ease, Ben asked, 'How's Young Tilly – and Granny?'

'Your Granny's as well as can be, and Tilly –' Grandpa's moustache widened into a smile. Then he glanced at the nurse, who was now putting Ben's snowdrops into water. He dropped his eyes; he coughed artificially.

'How's Tilly?' repeated Ben.

'Poor bitch,' said Grandpa, without raising his eyes. 'She's not so well.'

His words and manner were so evasive that Ben knew something was up. Suddenly he remembered Tilly vividly – saw her, in his mind's eye: liver-and-white, curly haired, fat, frolicsome, and – although she was called Young Tilly – getting old. Old for a dog, that is; but Ben did not know exactly how old, and he did not know at what age a dog such as Tilly might be expected to die. 'Is she – is she very ill?'

'Not ill at all, exactly.' Grandpa glanced round at the smart young nurse, who impressed and frightened him, and then looked directly at Ben. He curved his hand round his mouth to speak a private message. As Mr Fitch wrote with such difficulty, he always supposed that others would be as easily confused as himself by the spelling of words. 'She's going to pea-you-pea,' he confided.

'P – U – P?' Ben repeated, not understanding for a moment; but the nurse, pausing at the foot of the bed, exclaimed, 'Pup – have puppies! Now, isn't that nice! What breed will they be?'

Grandpa was flustered, but answered, 'The bitch is mostly spaniel, ma'am, but what her puppies will be like, we daren't say.' He turned to Ben: 'You remember that Toby you saw in the Codlings' canoe once? He's likely the father, as the time before, and he's mostly terrier.'

'Spaniel–terrier puppies – how very nice!'

'Puppies!' Ben said wonderingly.

'Aye, and us all thinking that sly bitch was past having puppies ever again! When they're born, you must come and see them, Ben.'

'There, Ben!' said the nurse. 'Whatever could be nicer?' She went out to fetch something.

'Puppies . . .' said Ben. Not dogs you could see only with your eyes shut; not dogs you could see only one side of, because they were worked in wool; not no-dogs. Real dogs, these – little flesh and blood and fur dogs – Tilly's puppies. He could not help saying, sadly, 'I wish . . .'

His grandfather picked up his hat and looked intently inside it, but seemed not to find there any suggestion of what he should say. He turned the hat round several times, and at last remarked, 'Your dad was saying this very day, over a piece of wedding-cake, that he thought you'd given up this idea of a dog in London. He said it was just impossible for you to have a dog where you live.'

'That's true,' said Ben. 'Just impossible to have a dog – even the smallest dog – impossible to have any size of dog at all.' And because he was remembering the one size of dog – the wonderful dog – that he had mistakenly thought it would be possible to have, and because he was still weak from illness, a tear went slowly down each cheek.

His grandfather saw the tears and looked away. 'You must come and see those puppies before they grow so big that we have to get rid of them. Your granny won't have 'em about the place longer than she can help.'

Ben tried to rally himself. He asked, 'Doesn't she like Tilly's having puppies?'

'Like? There's not much she can do about it. Your gran's a woman to reckon with; but, then, Tilly's female too. She's been a match for your granny this time.' Grandpa laughed at the joke of it; but Ben did not feel like laughing, and the nurse, coming in again, said he looked tired now. Grandpa took the hint and stood up, gripping his hat. 'Your granny said I was most particularly to hope you were better and give her love and say you're to come and stay as soon as you can, because country air is what you'll need.'

'There!' said the nurse.

'Thank you,' said Ben. His grandfather went, the nurse showing him the way out. And Ben turned his face into the pillow and – observed only by the little boy through the cot-bars – wept for a dog he could never have. That evening, when his mother slipped in for a few minutes with a piece of May's wedding-cake, Ben told her of Granny Fitch's invitation to stay, but not about Tilly's puppies.

For some time after the wedding, Ben had to stay in hospital. But he began to have more visitors, and not all from his family. The elderly woman whose car had knocked him down could hardly be counted even an acquaintance. Ben knew that he should apologize to her for the accident, admitting that it had all been his fault; and he did so. She began saying something about his walking into the road with his eyes shut, but then burst into tears. Ben tried to comfort her, but she continued to cry into her handkerchief. She left him a box of chocolates.

Then a policeman came. He sat with his helmet off, by Ben's bed, talking in a hushed voice. When Ben said that he was sorry and that the accident had been his fault, the policeman gently said, 'Yes.' He left Ben with a copy of the Highway Code – although nowhere in that is there any warning against trying to cross the road with your eyes shut.

Sooner or later, Ben knew, his mother would question him about his strange action on that terrible Christmas Eve. She would have connected his behaviour then with other behaviour, reported from school or observed by herself. In her anxiety she would press him for an explanation. He wanted to explain, but knew that he must not: his accident and May's wedding had been enough trouble to the family without reviving his old longing for a dog. And, unless he began by speaking of that, he could never explain.

At last, the question: 'Ben, dear, I want you to tell me something. On Christmas Eve, why were you trying to cross the road with your eyes shut?' He fobbed his mother off with some half-truth about aching eyes on that afternoon. 'But, no, Ben tell me . . .' He could not, because he must not.

However, when she cried a little, in a kind of despair, he went so far as to tell her one thing clearly: it would never happen again. He promised. With this simple but absolute assurance Mrs Blewitt had to allow herself to be satisfied.

Never again would Ben close his eyes to see a dog too small to be there: that dog had vanished at the traffic-lights on Christmas Eve, just as the woolwork dog had vanished one day on British Railways. Those two dogs gone, he was left with a third – no-dog: Ben had no dog.

CHAPTER 13

A Trip for Ben's Bones

Mrs Blewitt had been taken with the idea of Ben's going to his grandparents as soon as he was well enough. The hospital had suggested their convalescent home by the sea, but that sounded unhomely and bleak to Mrs Blewitt, especially at this time of year. And Ben wanted to go to the country, he said.

To begin with, Ben would need to have breakfast in bed and other attentions which old Mr and Mrs Fitch could not be expected to undertake. So, first of all, he would come to his home from hospital. Mrs Blewitt began to get ready for him the bedroom that had belonged to May and Dilys.

Mrs Blewitt was glad to be busy and particularly glad to welcome Ben home at this time. She missed May and Dilys more than she had ever foreseen in the excitement of the preparations for the wedding, the wedding itself, and the good-byes afterwards. Now there was no one to talk to about the affairs that particularly interest women and girls. Soon after the wedding, at tea-time, Mrs Blewitt had been about to speak of the Spring Sales, when she stopped herself with a cry: 'What's the use! With a houseful of men!' Mr Blewitt, Paul, and Frankie gazed at her dumbly, helplessly; and May and Dilys, in North London, were so far away.

Ben's return only made one more man in the house, but at least he was a convalescent — someone she could fuss over. In the morning, when Mr Blewitt had gone to work and the younger boys had gone to school, Mrs Blewitt would slip upstairs to Ben's bedroom and talk with him before starting her house-work; and Ben was glad of company, after all, in that large, new room all his own. He had no particular use for solitude nowadays.

Mrs Blewitt would bring Grandpa's letters upstairs to read aloud the bits that concerned Ben's coming visit. The last letter had a postscript: Mrs Blewitt studied it, baffled. 'I really can't think what it means, Ben, except that it's a message of some kind to you.'

'Let me see.' Ben read, in hurrying capitals: 'TELL BEN T PUPED (9).' He felt an emotion which he at once controlled. 'It must mean that Tilly has pupped – had nine puppies.'

'Well!' said Mrs Blewitt. 'Fancy! What a surprise!' She thought a moment, and then looked at Ben anxiously, but his face was expressionless.

'Do you think –' he began slowly, and his mother at once dreaded that he would want the impossible – to have one of the puppies in London. 'Do you think that I ought to tell Granny about losing the picture, when I go to stay?'

'What picture?' His mother had ceased to think of the woolwork picture soon after she had heard of its loss. She had never connected the picture with any dog that Ben might even impossibly hope to have.

'The picture of the little girl's dog called – called Chiquitito.'

'Oh, that!' Mrs Blewitt considered carefully. 'I don't think you really need to tell Granny, because after all the picture was given to you for your own – it was yours when you lost it. And telling Granny may make her sad, because the picture was a present to her from Uncle Willy. But, on the other hand, she's quite likely to ask you about the picture some time, and then, of course, you'd have to tell her. So, on the whole – yes, if I were you, I think I'd tell her before she asks.'

'I didn't think of all those reasons, but I did some-how think that I should have to tell her.' Ben sighed.

'Don't let Granny guess that the picture was never any good to you.'

'I won't.'

The day came for Ben's journey into the country.

His mother was coming with him to Castleford on a day excursion ticket, partly to see that his bones travelled safely, and partly because she always tried to manage one of her day trips to her parents between Christmas and Easter. Besides, she had a great deal to talk over with her mother.

The train reached Castleford in a fine February drizzle. Old Mr Fitch was waiting on the platform, with some shopping as usual, without Young Tilly, but with a large umbrella instead.

'We shan't need that, Pa,' Mrs Blewitt said, after kissing him, 'because we're going by taxi.'

'By taxi!' cried Grandpa. 'Why, whatever will your ma say!'

'Just this once, because of Ben's leg and ribs and collarbone. Bill gave me the money for it.' Mrs Blewitt insisted. In the splendour of a taxi, the three of them drove from Castleford to Little Barley and beyond and bumped cautiously up the driftway to the Fitches' front door.

They were, of course, much earlier than they would have been if they had waited to take the bus, and Granny Fitch was not expecting them. She was still in her wrap-round overall dress, and had been having a little sit-down in front of the fire. She had fallen asleep.

'Ma!' Mrs Blewitt called from the front door; and Mrs Fitch woke with a start and in some confusion of mind, so that – simply and solely, without time for thought – she saw her daughter. 'Lil!' she cried, and Lily Blewitt ran forward into her open arms. Ben hung back in the doorway, watching, feeling forgotten and odd for a moment, as he saw his own mother become the child of *her* mother.

Then Mrs Fitch held her daughter from her, adjusted her spectacles, and peered sharply at the large-faced clock. 'But you certainly didn't come by the bus.'

'We hired a car,' Mrs Blewitt said.

'*Hired a* – Joe!'

'It was Lily would do it,' Grandpa said hastily.

'But the expense!'

'Bill paid for it, Ma.'

'I don't care who paid for it,' said Granny; 'and you probably tipped the driver.'

'Bill gave me the money for that, too. It was all because of Ben, you know, Ma.'

'Ah, Ben . . .' Granny shifted her attention to Ben, who now came forward to be kissed. Then Granny, forgetting the taxi at least for the time being, bade Grandpa come in, and not let all the warmth out of the open door, and put the umbrella into the scullery, open if it were wet, furled if it were dry – which it was, but Grandpa was given no chance of saying so.

Grandpa did as he was told. As he went, he took from the corner of the kitchen-range a chipped enamel bowl from which rose a faint, warm, gravy smell. He saw Ben watching, and winked at him. Ben quietly left his mother and grandmother talking together and followed Grandpa into the scullery.

'Where are they? Where is she?'

Grandpa put the umbrella away, ran a little cold

water into the dog-stew to cool it, set it on the floor, and answered: 'The puppies are in the old sty down the garden, but Till's just outside now, if I know her.'

He opened the back-door, and there was Young Tilly waiting in the shelter of the porch. She came in with a preoccupied air – no more than an unsurprised wag of the tail even to Ben – and made straight for her dinner. She ate quickly, in large mouthfuls.

'She needs to eat well, with those nine greedy pups,' said Grandpa.

When she had finished, Tilly sat down, looked at Ben, moved her tail again, lay down, and seemed to go to sleep.

Ben was disappointed and a little shocked: 'Shouldn't she go back to them again, at once?' he asked.

'They're all right by themselves for a bit, and she knows it,' said Grandpa. 'She's a good mother, but she's not one of these young, fond ones. She feels a bit old for pups, I daresay, and she wearies of them. Then she stays here.'

'Shall we go and look at Tilly's puppies?' said Ben half to Tilly herself. She only opened one eye at her name, and did not respond. Grandpa, too, said that they had better postpone going until the rain had eased off a bit. Besides, Granny was calling to them both, asking whether they expected to have their dinners carried to them in the scullery.

Mrs Blewitt, with Grandpa's help, got the dinner, while Ben was made to rest on the sofa. Granny, after leaving full directions, went upstairs slowly but determinedly to change into the black silk dress which she had planned to wear for this visit.

They had hot-pot for dinner, followed by pancakes made by Mrs Blewitt. They were old Mr Fitch's favourite, but he could not manage the tossing. Then they had cups of tea and slices of home-made cake that Mrs Blewitt Blewitt had brought with her. And then the table was cleared and Mrs Blewitt spread out the wedding-photographs.

Granny pored over them: the bride and bridesmaid and page and bridegroom – 'I only hope he wears well' – and the guests. Grandpa took pleasure in pointing out any representations of himself – especially one which showed him wearing his hat. 'It wasn't wasted, then,' Granny commented.

'And this –' Mrs Blewitt ended up with a snapshot photograph. 'This is the house they're living in – May and Charlie, and Dilys, too, of course. They have a flat on this floor.'

Granny looked. 'Well, I suppose that's how people have to live in London.'

'But they're lucky, Ma; and I'm as pleased as they are about it, of course, except that – well, if only they weren't so far away!'

'That's what comes to you, when children grow up,' Granny said.

'And it isn't just that I miss them: they're still so young – it's Dilys I think of most, of course. They live in a nice place, really they do – hilly, so it's lovely air, for London; but it's all among strangers, and so far from us . . .'

Granny was listening closely, nodding. Mrs Blewitt said, 'Really, I've been thinking –' Then she glanced at Ben, who was also listening. She looked out of the window. 'It's stopped raining, Ben. Wouldn't you like a little stroll outside?'

Ben jumped up and looked expectantly at his grandfather. But first of all Grandpa had been looking at photographs, and now he seemed to be forgetfully settling down to a nap. Ben reminded him: 'Couldn't we go down the garden for a bit?'

'Ah?' said Grandpa, drowsily.

'Joe, Lil and I want to talk, so you'll take the boy now and show him those dratted puppies.'

And Grandpa and Ben went.

CHAPTER 14

Pig-sty in the Rain

They went to see Tilly's puppies. She did not want them to go; but, if they were going, she knew that her duty was to go too, and to go ahead. She went briskly but with a waddle, being incommoded by the swinging heaviness of the milk for her puppies.

The sty had once belonged to some pigs, but was now perfectly clean, with plenty of fresh straw on the concrete floor and a special lamp suspended low from one corner of the roof to give a gentle heat. Beneath this the puppies had all crawled and crowded together, and lay sleeping, a large, thick, sleek blob of multiple puppy-life.

Grandpa and Ben stooped under the corrugated iron roof of the sty and sat down on upturned buckets padded with folded sacking. Tilly had gone in front of them, but now she stood a little to one side and behind, very quietly. 'She's not keen on their knowing she's here at all,' said Grandpa. 'She knows they'll be squeaking and pushing after her milk, once they do know. And they're none of 'em starving.'

Grandpa plunged his fingers into the heap of puppies and brought one out at random. He dropped it into Ben's cupped hands. It just filled them – as a full grown Chihuahua might have done, Ben thought. 'Chiquitito!' he said softly.

Ben felt perfect happiness. He shifted the puppy into one hand – which it slightly overflowed – in order to be able to stroke it with the back of the forefinger of his other hand. Then he put it down and gently picked up another. The puppies varied in size, but all were sleek-coated and fat. Their colours varied, too: liver-and-white, like Tilly herself, black and white, or mostly black, or mostly brown. One was as brown as if a gravy tureen had just been emptied over him; another was all-over brown, too, but lighter.

Tilly watched Ben handling her puppies, but she did not seem to mind. If he held a puppy out to her, she began licking it with thoroughness. This was her habit with any puppy that came within easy reach – although she was so unsystematic that she might spring-clean the same one several times running and leave others untouched.

When Ben had held each puppy in turn, he wanted to see Tilly with them all. 'Come on, then, old girl!' Grandpa coaxed; but Tilly groaned, wagged her tail, and would not budge from her distance. At last, with Grandpa always pushing her gently from behind, she reluctantly got up and waded forward into her little sea of puppies. At once it broke round her in eager, ruthless welcome. Puppies cried and snorted and pushed and trod each other down in a soft, squashy stampede to reach her teats. Tilly gave herself up and subsided among them. She licked some convenient ones, but otherwise paid no attention – as they paid no attention to her lickings. Over the pulsing bodies of nine hard-sucking pups, she looked at Grandpa and Ben, patiently, mildly, and she yawned.

'Well, there you are, boy,' Grandpa said, as though the interest were exhausted. It was, for him. He said he was going back to the house, before the hard rim of the bucket ended by giving him sciatica, and anyway it was beginning to rain again.

Ben stayed on, alone, to watch. He liked being in the sty with the rain sounding on the iron roof just above his head, and the dim, warm light from the lamp, and the smell of straw and puppies. He liked being alone with Till and her feeding puppies. Sometimes he could be of help. He brought home a puppy that had strayed or been pushed beyond Tilly's tail and was whimpering for lost food. He righted another puppy that – still sucking – had somehow got turned

upside down. He unburied another – always sucking –
that had been quite trampled under and out of sight by
the others.

He could bear to leave them only when he had to –
when his mother called from the house for tea. He
stood up to go, and at once Young Tilly heaved herself
up and began to walk carefully away from her mother-
hood. Most of the puppies, satiated with milk, had
already given up sucking in favour of sleep. The
few remaining fell from their mother like over-ripe
pears – which by now they rather resembled in shape.
Almost without complaint they crawled back with the
others into the puppy-heap under the warmth of the
lamp.

Ben went in to tea with Tilly at his heels. Granny
did not notice the dog because she was looking at the
boy. She and his mother had both stopped speaking
and were considering him in a way that made him
know they had been talking of him. 'He certainly
looks as if he could do with better air all the time,'
Granny said, as if concluding some discussion. The
remark was senseless to Ben, and he forgot it at
once. His mind and all his sensations were dazed,
drugged, utterly overwhelmed by puppies. But the
remark had been of importance, and helped towards
important decisions of which Ben knew nothing until
later.

After tea, Mrs Blewitt caught the bus back to Castleford and then the train back to London. That night,

after Paul and Frankie had gone to bed, she said: 'I had a good long talk with Ma this afternoon, Bill, about things.'

'Things?' Mr Blewitt was listening to his wife but watching the television screen.

'You know, our being so far away from Dilys and May and her Charlie, and this house being really bigger than we need since they've gone –'

'Is it?'

'Yes,' Mrs Blewitt said firmly. 'Oh, and other things! Anyway, I've had half an idea in my head, and I told Ma this afternoon. She thought it was a good idea.' Mrs Blewitt began to explain.

Soon there was no doubt that Mr Blewitt was listening, with increasing amazement. He leaned forward, switched off the television set, and turned to face his wife.

'But, Lil, have you taken leave of your senses! First a street-accident, and then a wedding, and then – then *this*! You take after your ma for energy, Lil, and that's a fact! Are we never to be allowed any peace and quiet?'

Mrs Blewitt soothed him. This was only an idea; there was no need to take any decision yet. (Mr Blewitt leaned forward to the television-switch.) But the idea had many advantages. (Mr Blewitt sank back again with a groan.) She had seen those clearly this afternoon when she had talked things over with Ma. 'As Ma said, look what good it would do Ben, for one! He'd have better air – we all should!'

'I suppose it all comes down to this,' said Mr Blewitt. 'You and your ma have made a plan. So it's as good as decided.' Poor Mr Blewitt! He hated changes and moves.

CHAPTER 15

To Have and Not to Have

*B*en was breathing a great deal of the sleepy puppy-air of the Fitches' pig-sty, for he visited the puppies several times a day; and he was feeling better and better.

During his stay, the puppies began to be weaned. Grandpa started by persuading them to drink cow's milk from a dish as well as – soon, instead of – Tilly's milk. None of the puppies was interested in cow's milk at first, and Ben's job was to accustom them to the idea. He planted them round the rim of the milk-dish, brought them back to it when they wandered away, lifted them out of it when they began paddling across, and gently pushed their muzzles into it. Gradually, in a muddled way, they gained a taste for the new drink, first by licking it off the coats of those who had fallen in, at last by lapping from the dish. When they began to feed as fast-growing puppies, they made more mess in their straw, and Ben took on the job of cleaning the sty out regularly and laying fresh straw.

In their daily company, handling them often, Ben came to know each puppy well. He gave them their names, which Grandpa – who hadn't thought of names until Ben came – adopted. Two were Punch and Judy, because they resembled the Codlings' Toby in colouring; two others, coloured liver-and-white, were called Mat and Tilda, after Tilly (whose real name was Matilda); then there was Midnight, all black; and Cloudy, who could not make up his mind whether to be black or white or even a proper grey; and Spot – whose name needed no explanation once you saw him; and Gravy, an all-over dark brown.

That was eight, and now Ben's invention began to fail. About the ninth puppy there was nothing distinctive, unless perhaps he was the smallest – but he might grow out of that. His colour was like Gravy's only lighter. Ben, searching his mind for an apt name, stared at the puppy: 'He's brown . . .'

'A very handy name, too,' Grandpa said heartily. 'I like Brown.' And so – with Ben's acceptance of his grandfather's mistake – the ninth puppy was named Brown. Once he was called that, you could only wonder that he might ever have been called anything else.

Old Mrs Fitch had never seen the puppies – didn't want to, she said. She grumbled, too, at Ben's spending so much time with them – 'cooped up in a pigsty – what would his mother say?'

Ben heard from his mother regularly. In one letter Mrs Blewitt reported a Sunday visit that the family had paid to May and Charlie and Dilys in their new home. She had thoroughly enjoyed a proper talk with her two daughters, and had come to the final conclusion that their district was the best in all London to live in. For one thing, it was so far from the river-fogs and damps of the Blewitts' part of South London. The air of North London was so pure, she wrote; but there! Ben was breathing fresh country air for the present, anyway. When old Mrs Fitch had had that read to her, she began sending Ben for afternoon walks along the driftway.

The driftway, smitten by winter, was cold, lifeless. It was hard to think of Grandpa finding even half a dozen early snowdrops there; he had known where to look. There seemed nothing now. Last year's grass lay rotting and tangled round the feet of melancholy, broken-armed skeletons of what might once have been cow-parsley, meadowsweet, teasel. The hedges were without leaves, so that Ben could see through them to the cold, raw earth of ploughed fields; and winds blew over the fields and draughtily through the hedges.

Ben trudged along because he had to, and Tilly – when she would come at all – followed spiritlessly, her head drooping. She did not fuss over her puppies, but her thoughts must always be with them.

They never went further than the driftway bridge over the Say. The river, swollen with winter waters, was fast-moving and dangerous-looking, and grey and cold. No one would want to bathe in that. The willow-tree beside which Ben had undressed was a bleak landmark in a desolate marsh.

Leaning over the handrail of the bridge, Ben felt a melancholy creeping over him, fixing him to this spot. There was, of course, no Mexican volcano in sight; but here he felt truly, as he had felt in his nightmares, that he had no dog. He had lost the woolwork dog; he had lost the visionary dog. He might tend and fondle Tilly's puppies but none of them was his. He named them for other owners; not one of them was his Chiquitito. He had no dog.

At last, Tilly, who had been sitting beside him on the cold, damp concrete of the bridge, got up and began plodding back the way they had come, unwilling to keep him company any longer. Ben turned and followed her. Dusk came by the end of the afternoon, and, as they neared home, they often saw the lit windows of the Yellow Salden bus as it passed along the main road. Ben could see the passengers inside looking out over the lonely, wintry landscape, glad that they were not there.

Then Ben, not even having the heart to call at the pig-sty on the way, went drearily in to tea. After tea he always read to his grandmother, his grandfather listening too. Then, bed.

Ben had been waiting for a good time, preferably when his grandmother was alone, to tell her of the loss of the woolwork picture. He chose a Sunday evening after his walk and after old Mr Fitch had gone off to the chapel-service in Little Barley. Ben was left to keep his grandmother company. He had been reading the Bible aloud; he broke off, and went on again at once: 'You know Uncle Willy's picture . . .'

He paused, waiting; but his grandmother, who had been listening with her eyes shut, did not open them now. Ben wondered whether she thought that this was all part of the Book of Jeremiah, or whether she had fallen asleep – but that was unlikely. Just as he was preparing to repeat what he had said, she opened her eyes. 'What happened to Willy's picture?'

'I lost it.' He told her when and where.

She said nothing.

'I'm sorry,' Ben said. 'I know it was a present to you from Uncle Willy.'

'And then a present to you, but you didn't take to it.'

'It wasn't exactly that, but –'

'You wanted a real dog.'

'Yes.'

'You still do.'

It was Ben's turn to be silent.

'That Joe should never have promised you a dog.'

'Please!' said Ben. 'It doesn't make any difference now, truly.'

'A promise was broken.'

Another silence. Ben wondered if he should go on reading aloud, but his grandmother did not ask him to do so. She had shut her eyes again. Perhaps she was really asleep this time.

Ben closed the Bible and put it aside. He glanced at the clock. Grandpa would be home soon, and then it would be time for bed. Always, before bed, he tried to slip out for a last look at the puppies. He was pretty sure that Grandpa guessed where he went, but not Granny. He glanced at her now and decided that she really was asleep. He tiptoed into the scullery and out through the back door.

He never hurried in saying good night to the puppies. He held each one separately, bending his face over it, saying its name: 'Midnight ... Tilda ... Cloudy ... Brown ...'

He became aware of some difference behind him, where the entrance to the pig-sty was. The flow of air from the outside was blocked by some body – a silent presence – in the doorway. For a moment Ben was frightened – too frightened to move or to show his awareness in any way. His grandfather would have hailed him, 'Well, boy!' at once – he always did; and the only other person it could rightfully be was his grandmother, but she never stirred out of doors in this weather, and in the dark, too.

But, looking out of the corner of his eye, Ben could see – just within the light from the lamp – a pair of black buttoned shoes and grey cotton stockings above them: this was his grandmother.

She was standing at the entrance of the sty – probably stooping to watch him. He did not know why she watched, and could only suppose that she would be angry with him for being here yet again, and so late. He waited for her to speak, and in the meantime went on fondling the puppies, pretending not to know that she was there.

But she did not speak. After a while there was a little squeaking sound from her shoes, which meant that she had turned away from the sty to go back to the house. Ben gave her plenty of time, because she would hobble so slowly, and it was dark. Then he followed. When he got indoors, she was sitting in her chair by the fire, with her eyes shut, as though she had never moved from it. Only, she was breathing a little heavily, and there was mud on the toe of one shoe.

Ben, not seeking trouble, sat down quietly, but then did not know what to do. He looked at his grandmother again, and found her eyes open and fixed upon him.

'Shall I go on reading, Granny?'

'To the end of the chapter, please.' He began to look for the place again. 'Ben, you were promised a dog. The promise ought to have been kept – kept properly. We ought to have done that. So, now, one of those puppies is yours by right.'

'Mine – oh!' For a moment Ben was dazzled by the amazing thought that he owned one of Tilly's puppies. Which? – for they would let him choose. He was indeed dazzled, for his mind's eye followed a rapid sequence of colours: liver-and-white, black and white, cloudy grey, dark brown, light brown – He stopped there because the puppy called Brown was the one nearest to Chiquitito-coloured. He would choose Chiquitito-Brown for his own, and together – he and this second Chiquitito, as small and as brave as the first – together they would roam London –

Then he remembered: if he were offered all the dogs in the world, he could not accept one. He could not keep a dog in London, where there was nowhere to exercise it, nowhere for it to run free.

His grandmother had been watching him – watching the expression on his face change from one moment to the next, with the change of his thought.

'Yes, but –' Ben said heavily.

'Yes,' said his grandmother. 'That's how things are, and I'm sorry for it.' As she hated to wrap her meaning in politeness or irony or anything but its own truth, Ben knew that she was truly sorry. 'And now, boy, go on reading from the Book of the Prophet Jeremiah.'

CHAPTER 16

A View from a Hill-top

*H*e was Ben's, then; and not Ben's.

He was not an extraordinary puppy as yet, and he was much darker than the true Chiquitito-fawn. Nevertheless, Ben hung over him, loving him, learning him, murmuring the name that should have been his: 'Chiquitito . . .'

Ben was there when Chiquitito-Brown barked for the first time. Standing four-square and alone, the puppy's body suffered a spasm of muscular contraction which released itself when he opened his jaws. The open mouth was just about the size to take the bulk of, say, a finger-end. From this aperture issued – small, faint, but unmistakeable – a bark. Then Chiquitito-Brown closed his mouth and looked round, quivering back in alarm at the sound he had heard.

For the puppy, more like his mother than his heroic namesake, was not brave. That would have to come later, Ben reassured himself; and in the meantime – 'You're really Chiquitito,' Ben told him again and again, trying to teach him his new name and the new nature that went with it. At least the puppy was still very, very small.

Grandpa, of course, did not know of the re-naming; but he guessed, from Ben's favouritism, which would have been the boy's choice among all the puppies. On the last day of Ben's visit, he asked: 'And what shall I do with Brown, since you can't take him back to London with you?'

'What will you do with the others?'

'Offer them round to the family – your uncles and aunties,' Grandpa said. 'And those pups that aren't taken that way – we shall sell 'em off if we can, give 'em away if we can't.'

'Then you'll have to do the same with him.' Ben held Chiquitito-Brown squirming between his hands for the last time. He put his face against the puppy's head, breathed his good-bye.

And, on the evening after Ben's departure, Grandpa squared up to the table and wrote round to the families offering a gift of a puppy to each. He did not bother to ask the family so far away in Canada, of course, nor the Blewitts themselves.

After some time he began to get the replies. Ben, at home again in London, heard that an uncle who had settled in the Fens, the other side of Castleford, would take one puppy – Midnight; and another – Gravy – was going to the aunt who had married a man in Essex.

Ben laid down the letter which had brought this news, and thought: two puppies gone – that left seven to be disposed of, Chiquitito-Brown being one.

Ben, quite well again now, was back at school, thus altogether resuming normal life. He was never seen with his eyes shut in the daytime; he was never found in strange abstractions of thought. He was a perfectly ordinary boy again – only, perhaps, a little dispirited. But his mother was satisfied that the change to North London would work wonders in Ben, and in them all. For the Blewitt family were going to move house: Mrs Blewitt's idea had really been a plan, as her husband had grasped, and now it had been decided upon and would be carried out.

'But I've to be within reach of my job, mind that,' said Mr Blewitt. Mrs Blewitt pointed out that, for someone with Mr Blewitt's kind of Underground job, there wasn't much to choose between living towards the southern end of the Northern Line, as they did at present, and living towards the northern end of the same Line, as they would be doing.

'Yes,' said Mr Blewitt. Then he closed his eyes: 'But the upheaval – leaving somewhere where we were settled in so well.' Mrs Blewitt pointed out that the departure of May and Dilys had already unsettled them: the house had become too big for them. (Perhaps, if the Blewitts had not been so used to squeezing seven in, five would not have seemed too few in the space. Or perhaps they would not have seemed too few if Mrs Blewitt had not been thinking of the comfort of living nearer to her daughters.)

And besides, Mrs Blewitt went on, the *air* –

'I've heard enough about the flavour of that air,' her husband said with finality. 'If we go, we go. That's all there is to it, Lil.'

'We go,' Mrs Blewitt said happily, as though all problems were settled now. So the rest of the family were told. Frankie – who took after his mother, everyone said – was delighted at the thought of the excitement of removal. Paul only worried about his pigeon: he did not yet realize that birds can be as cordial in North London as in South. Ben said nothing, thought nothing, felt nothing – didn't care.

His keenest interest, but sombre, was in the news that Grandpa sent in his letter-postscripts. Old Mr Fitch was now getting rid of the rest of Tilly's puppies, one by one, in the Little Barley neighbourhood. Jem Perfect of Little Barley was taking one – Punch; and Constable Platt another – Judy. That left five, Chiquitito-Brown among them.

'It's only a question of time,' said Mrs Blewitt. 'If anyone can hear of the right kind of house or flat for us, it will be Charlie Forrester. He's on the spot; he's in the know. We only have to be patient.' She glowed with hope.

Another weekly letter came from the Fitches. 'Here you are, Ben,' said Mrs Blewitt, 'there's a message for you again.'

The postscript read:

TELL B MRS P TOKE TILDA

That meant that the Perkinses from next door had taken the puppy called Tilda. It would be nice for Young Tilly to have her own daughter living next door. And that left four puppies, Chiquitito-Brown still among them. Ben suddenly realized that his grand-father must be keeping his – Ben's – puppy to the end: he intended to give him away the last of all. But, in the end, he would have to give him.

The Blewitts were going to look at a family-sized flat that Charlie Forrester had found for them in North London. It was a house-conversion job, he said, and wouldn't be ready for some time but it might suit them. There was even a back-garden, or yard, nearly fifteen foot square. As the only viewing day was Sunday, all the family went.

There seemed nothing special about the district – just streets leading into streets leading into streets – or about the house itself – just like all the other houses in all the other streets: Ben himself could not even dislike the street or the house, outside or in.

His mother was disappointed at it. 'Only two medium sized bedrooms, and a little box of a room where Ben would sleep.'

'I thought his present bedroom was too big,' said Mr Blewitt.

'But this is poky.'

'It would just take Ben's bed and leave him room to get into it, anyway,' said May, who had come with her Charlie. She was taking them all back to their flat for tea afterwards.

'Well, what do *you* think, Ben?' Mrs Blewitt asked.

'I don't mind,' said Ben. He was indifferent; and Paul and Frankie were bored – they were scuffling in empty rooms, irritating their father, whose nerves were on edge. He sent all three out of the house.

They wandered together from one street to the next and so came to a road that was less of a side-street than the others. The two younger boys pricked their ears at the whirring and rattling sound of roller-skates, and took that direction. Ben did not care for the sport, but he followed the others – as the eldest, he was always supposed to be partly in charge.

Boys and even a few girls were roller-skating in zigzags down a wide, asphalted footway that sloped to the road, with a system of protective barriers across at that end. Paul and Frankie recognized this as ideal skating ground, fast but safe. They settled down to watch. Soon, Ben knew, they would try to borrow someone's skates for a turn, and they might succeed. Anyway, they would be occupied for some time.

Ben went on, chiefly because he did not care for all the company and noise. He climbed the sloping way, crossed a railway bridge, and came out by a low brick building. It was probably a sports pavilion, for it looked out over a grassed space, part of which was a football ground. To one side there was a children's playground with a paddling pool and easy swings. Asphalted paths skirted the whole open space, which sloped steadily still upwards to a sky-line with trees.

Ben left the asphalt and struck directly up over the grass towards the highest point in sight. As he climbed he became aware of how high he must be getting. He took the last few yards of the ascent walking backwards to see the view in the direction from which he had come – southwards, right over London.

He thought that he had never seen a further, wider view of London and, indeed, there is hardly a better one. The extremity of the distance was misted over, but Ben could quite easily distinguish the towers of Westminster and even Big Ben itself. The buildings of London advanced from a misty horizon right to the edge of the grassy space he had just traversed. The houses stopped only at the railway-line. He could see the bridge he had crossed; and now he saw a spot of scarlet moving over it. That would be Frankie in his red jersey, and the spot of blue following him would be Paul. He could see them hesitate, questingly, and then the red and blue moved swiftly in a bee-line to the children's playground. Well, that would certainly keep them busy and safe until May's tea-time.

Ben had reached his summit facing backwards – southwards, and he had looked only at that view. Now he turned to see the view in the opposite direction.

There were buildings, yes, some way to the right and to the left, for this was still within the sprawl of London; but, between, there were more trees, more grass – a winding expanse.

So – it went on.

Ben stared, immobile, silent. People strolled by him, people sat on benches near him, no one appeared aware of the importance to Ben Blewitt of what he now saw. Even if the place were no bigger than it seemed on this first entry, it was already big enough for his purposes. *And it went on.* He had a premonition – a conviction – of great green spaces opening before him, inviting him. He felt it in his bones – the bones of his legs that now, almost as in a dream, began to carry him forward into the view. Asphalted paths, sports pavilions, and all the rest were left behind as he left the high slopes of Parliament Hill for the wilder, hillocky expanses of Hampstead Heath.

CHAPTER 17

The Real Question

Of course, being a Londoner, he had heard of Hampstead Heath, and several times recently Charlie, May, or Dilys had mentioned its nearness to their part of North London; but Ben had paid no particular attention. He had even been on the Heath once, years before, when he was very little. Mr and Mrs Blewitt had taken their three eldest children (Paul and Frankie were not yet born) to the August Bank Holiday Fair, held on part of the Heath. There had been merry-go-rounds and coconut shies and crowds through which May and Dilys had dragged him, each holding one of his hands. That was really all he remembered.

This time there was no fair, no dense crowds of people: he was on his own on the open Heath.

For a while he would follow a path, never asphalted or gravelled, never ruled straight to any plan. The ways across Hampstead Heath are mostly tracks that go where Londoners' feet have made them go, muddy in winter, dusty and scuffed in summer. Then he would cut across grass and through bushes to reach some point of vantage: there were no notices prohibiting it. The grass on Hampstead Heath is tough, tousled, wild, free – green and springy at the time of year when Ben trod it; later, brown and trampled and tired, longing for the repose of winter, whose damps also rot away the litter left by careless people. The trees and bushes on the Heath seem to grow where they themselves have chosen, and in irregular shapes comfortable to themselves. Ben liked them like that.

There are slippery slopes and potholes, which the wary avoid, for fear of twisting an ankle; but Ben was agile. There are marshy places in hollows, with no notices warning people that they may get their feet wet. Ben got his feet wet, and did not care.

He wandered up and down, round and round, farther and farther. He came to the slow, wide dip of heathland beyond which Kenwood House presents its bland front. He stared, and then turned away, and on. Wherever he went he saw people – plenty of people on such a fine afternoon; but the Heath is never overcrowded. The sun was hot for the time of year, and some people were even lying on the grass: elderly men on spread-out waterproofs, Sunday newspapers over their faces; young lovers in their embraces, careless of rheumatism from damp grass or dazzle from the sun. A mother sat knitting while her baby practised walking. A boy flew a kite. Children at play called to each other over wide spaces. And Ben saw dogs – dogs that ran freely, barking without correction. You were not even sure to whom any particular dog belonged until a distant shout recalled him.

Ben roved on, by a stretch of water and men fishing in it and a public house beyond. Then he climbed a slope up to a road and traffic – traffic that moved on all sides of a pond where fathers and children sailed boats. Beyond this a flagstaff and flag reared itself up; and beyond again was more grass, with bushes, sloping away to more tree-tops. So the Heath still went on.

But Ben paused. From the feel of his legs, he knew that he had come a long way, and he knew that the time was late from the feel of his stomach, which was empty for May's tea. Besides, he had seen enough already; the place was big enough – vast and wild. And it still went on.

He turned round, set off impetuously back, realized that he did not know the way after all his indirect wanderings and then saw the keeper – the first he had seen since entering upon the Heath. He must be some kind of park-keeper, from his brown uniform and the metal badge on the front of his hat. He had just strolled up one of the paths and was now standing a moment, watching the people or nothing in particular.

In the ordinary course of things, Ben would not have asked his way of a park-keeper. He did not like them. But now he wanted to lead up to a more important – a vital question which only a park-keeper could answer with authority.

He edged up to him: 'Please!'

'Yes?'

'Please, could you tell me the way to get back?' Ben described the railway bridge, the sports pavilion and playground, the grassy hill –

'You want Parliament Hill,' said the keeper, and pointed his direction out to him.

Ben thanked him, set off slowly, came back, and said: 'Please!'

'What is it now?'

But Ben lacked the courage for the real question. He invented a substitute: 'I wanted to know what flag it is up there – please.'

'It's our flag – the London County Council house-flag.'

'Oh. Why is it flying today?'

'We fly it every day, unless we fly the Union Jack instead. Anything else you want to know?'

Yes, indeed, if only he dared ask; but – 'No, thank you – no – at least, that is – what do you fly the Union Jack for, then?'

'Special occasions: anniversary of the accession of the Queen; Queen's birthday; Queen's wedding-day; birthday of Queen Elizabeth the Queen Mother; opening of Parliament –' He was slowing up in his list, eyeing Ben.

'Thank you very much,' said Ben.

Now or never: if he hesitated again, the keeper would decide that he was thinking up questions just to be impertinent. He would ask Ben why he didn't go home, now that he knew the direction. He would send him packing, with the really important question unasked, unanswered.

So, for the third time, and very quickly this time: 'Please!'

'Now, look here –'

'Please – *please*: can anyone take a dog on the Heath and just let him run free? Are there no rules saying that dogs mustn't do things?'

The park-keeper looked horrified. 'No rules – no by-laws? Of course there are by-laws! We can't have dogs getting out of control on the Heath.' As the keeper spoke, two dogs – one in pursuit of the other – tore up the path on which he was standing. He stepped slightly aside to let them pass, never removing his gaze from Ben.

'But how exactly must they not get out of control?' Ben asked.

'Biting people, mainly.'

Well, that was quite a reasonable rule: Ben began to feel cheerful.

'Mind you, there's one pretty severe regulation for some dogs. Have you a dog?'

It was the same difficult question that the librarian had once asked – difficult, now, in a different way. 'I *own* a dog,' said Ben; 'but I haven't got it.'

'What kind?'

Ben thought of Chiquitito-Brown, and of his parent-
age. 'It's difficult to say. You see –'

'Is it greyhound breed?'

Ben thought of Tilly and then of Toby; either of
them might have some greyhound-blood coursing secretly in their veins, but on the whole – 'No, not
greyhound.'

'Your dog's lucky. On Hampstead Heath greyhounds
must wear muzzles.'

'And other breeds of dogs, and just mongrels?'

'Needn't. Provided they're kept under reasonable
control, of course, as I've said.'

The same two dogs as before tore past again in the
same pursuit, except that one was gaining on the other.

'And no leads?' asked Ben.

'No. I've told you: provided they're kept under
control.'

A few yards from where Ben and the keeper stood,
one of the two dogs had caught the other up, and they
were now rolling and growling in a play-fight. Such
an incident was beneath the keeper's notice. He said to
Ben: 'Just remember, always under proper control on
this Heath. And now cut along home the way I told
you to go.'

Ben went running, light as air from the joy he felt.

He was very late for tea, of course. Everyone had
finished, except for Paul and Frankie, who were being
held back from the remains saved for Ben. Everybody
was cross with him: Paul and Frankie for his having
come back at all, the others for his being so late. He

explained that he had been walking around and forgotten the time.

They resumed conversation, and, when he had a moment free from eating cold, butter-soggy toast, Ben asked about the flat seen that afternoon: had they decided to take it?

'Well . . .' said Mrs Blewitt.

In short, they hadn't decided. May and Dilys said it was a good flat, not expensive, especially for those parts and Charlie said that if they didn't take it, someone else soon would; and Mr Blewitt said that they might as well move there, if they had to move at all. But Mrs Blewitt was full of doubts. The place was poky, for one thing.

'I didn't see anything wrong with it,' said Ben. 'You said that little room was poky, but I didn't think so. I'd like to sleep there: I like it: I like the house: I like where it is.' He wanted them to know; he wanted to do all that lay within his poor means: '*I'd like to live there.*'

'My!' said May; and Charlie said, 'You'll soon have a voice as loud and clear as Big Ben's!'

Everyone laughed at that; and Ben was glad that he had not spoken of wanting to live within reach of the Heath. They might have laughed at that, too. His family were not unsympathetic; but they would not see the overwhelming importance of living near the Heath. Paul and Frankie might have a glimmering of understanding; but not his mother and father. His mother wanted a flat or house comfortable for the family and easy to run; his father wanted somewhere handy for his job. Of course, they would enjoy going on the Heath occasionally – on fine Sunday afternoons for a family stroll, for instance. But Ben would be on the Heath every morning before breakfast, every evening after school, every weekend, every day of the holidays. The Heath was a necessity to Ben – to Ben and his dog, the second and no less wonderful Chiquitito. Tilly's puppy.

But nothing at all was decided yet.

There was only one more thing Ben could do to help forward his hopes. That evening, at home, he wrote a postcard to his grandfather: 'Please keep my puppy for me. Will write more later.' He posted the card on Monday morning; it would arrive with the Fitches on Tuesday.

On Tuesday Mrs Blewitt received a letter written by her father, with a long message for Ben. No less than three of Tilly's remaining puppies had been disposed of: Judy, to the caretaker of the chapel in Little Barley; Cloudy to Mrs Perkins's mother in Yellow Salden; and Mat to a friend of Bob Moss's in Castleford.

That left only one puppy: Chiquitito-Brown.

'Chiquitito!' Ben whispered to himself, catching his breath at the narrowness of the shave; but he knew that he had been in time. His card must have crossed Grandpa's letter in the post. Grandpa would be warned by now.

That Tuesday morning old Mr Fitch read Ben's postcard aloud to his wife. Neither of them questioned keeping the puppy: it was Ben's. 'As long as he takes it away some day,' said Granny. 'That's all.'

'Well,' said Grandpa, 'it sounds to me as if he hopes to keep a dog in London, after all.' The idea gripped him: he smiled; his fingers tapped a cheerful beat on the postcard; he was brimming with optimism and happiness for Ben.

'All I hope is that he's not due for any disappointment,' said Mrs Fitch.

CHAPTER 18

'Bring Mrzzl for Jurney'

When Ben had been much younger – and Frankie probably still did this; perhaps even Paul – he used to hold his breath when he wanted something badly. He held it, for instance, when they were passing a plate of cakes round and there was only one of his favourite kind.

Now, when he wanted something more than he had ever wanted anything else in all his life, he felt as if he were holding his breath for days on end – for weeks.

His parents could still not make up their minds to take the flat they had seen that Sunday. It was not exactly what Mrs Blewitt had hoped for, she said. On the other hand, she had to admit that other flats were usually more expensive, or less convenient, or farther from May and Dilys. She admitted all that; and the admitting made her incline increasingly – but still hesitantly – towards taking the flat. Slowly, slowly she was veering round to it.

Ben listened to his parents' discussions. He saw the way that things were going; but he could not be sure that they were going that way fast enough. For Charlie Forrester had said that if the Blewitts did not take that particular flat, then somebody else would, soon enough. The Blewitts would lose their chance, through indecision and delay.

So Ben held his breath. He would not allow himself to show emotion – almost, to feel it. He determined not to count upon having a dog; he would not hope for a dog – even think of a dog. Yet, equally, he could not think of anything else properly at all. The dog that he chased absolutely from his thoughts in the daytime stole back at night, into his dreams: Tilly's tiny, pale brown puppy, who was also the minute – the minimal, fawn-coloured, intrepid, and altogether extraordinary Chihuahua named Chiquitito. Ben called him by that name as, in his dreams, they roamed Hampstead Heath together.

Even when Mrs Blewitt came to her decision, and, after all, the flat had not been snapped up yet by anyone else, so the Blewitts could have it – even then, Ben hardly dared breathe freely. So much might still go wrong.

But when the date of house-removal was actually fixed, and Mrs Blewitt was altering the curtains to fit the new windows, Ben said: 'By the way, I could have a dog when we're living there, couldn't I?'

Mrs Blewitt stopped whirring the sewing-machine. 'Ben!'

'Really, I could!' Ben explained what his mother had never realized – the closeness of the new home to the Heath. He could exercise a dog properly, easily, regularly; he himself would see to its feeding and washing; he would see that it did not bring mud into the house or leave hairs there – Ben over-rode all objections to a dog even before they could be made.

'But, Ben!' said his mother. 'If you *can* have a dog, I want you to. In spite of your granny's scolding, we always had a dog when we were children. A family of children should have a dog, if possible.' Ben suddenly leaned over the sewing-machine and kissed his mother. 'Mind you! You must talk to your father, of course.'

And she went back to her whirring.

When Mr Blewitt came in, he saw the justice of Ben's case: there was no reason why Ben should not keep a dog in the part of London they were moving to. But where would Ben get his dog, and how much – on top of all the expenses of house-removal – would it cost?

'Nothing,' said Ben, 'because Grandpa and Granny

have been keeping one of Tilly's puppies for me, just in case. They'll give it to me as soon as I ask for it, for a birthday present.'

'Your birthday's some way ahead yet.'

'Well, really, it would be for my last birthday.'

'And, although the dog will belong to Ben,' Mrs Blewitt said, 'all the family will enjoy it.'

'As we all enjoyed Frankie's white mouse when it last got loose – you especially, Lil.'

'Oh, no!' Ben said eagerly. 'It won't be like having a white mouse – truly.'

'I daresay not. Bigger, for one thing.' But, in spite of his sardonic speech, Mr Blewitt accepted the idea, as his wife had done; and Paul and Frankie eagerly welcomed it.

'What is your dog like?' Frankie asked. They had not seen any of Tilly's puppies.

'Very, very small.'

'When you last saw it, Ben,' said Mrs Blewitt. 'Remember that puppies grow fast.' But Ben paid no attention.

'Go on, Ben,' said Paul. 'What colour is it?'

'Brown – a lightish brown.' He hesitated, then said boldly: 'Well, really, a pinky-fawn.' That was the colour it must be – Chiquitito-coloured.

'Go on.'

'And it's very bold and brave.'

Mr Blewitt asked what Ben was going to call his dog. Again he hesitated (but not because he had not

made up his mind), and at once the others began
making suggestions: Rover. Plucky, Wagger –

'No,' said Ben. 'None of those. He's got his own
name already.'

'Well, what?'

He knew that they would object, so he began,
'Well, Grandpa has been calling him Brown –'

'Sensible,' said Mr Blewitt.

'But his real name is Chiquitito.'

A hush fell. 'Chicky *what*?' asked Mr Blewitt. He did
not remember – none of them did – that this had been
the name on the back of the woolwork picture.

'– Tito,' said Ben. 'Chiquitito.'

'You can't call him that, Ben,' said Mr Blewitt. He
meant that the thing was – not forbidden, of course –
just impossible. 'His name is Brown.'

'Chiquitito,' said Ben.

Then they all pointed out to Ben what an unhandy,
absurd, unthinkable name that was for a dog. They
argued with him and laughed at him. He stuck by
what he had said. In the end they gave up without
giving way, and they forgot the dog for the time
being. After all, it had been decided that Ben should
not fetch his dog until after the house-removal.

The Blewitts moved house. When all the bumping and
muddle and dust and crossness were over, and they were
really settled into the new flat, Ben – with his parents'
agreement – wrote to his grandfather and grandmother.
He arranged to go down for the day to fetch his dog.

Ben travelled down to Castleford alone, on a day-excursion ticket. He took a carrier-bag of home-made cooking from his mother, and his father had bought him a dog's lead and a leather collar with a silver name-and-address plate on it. His grandfather had asked him to bring the lead and the collar, and he had also written at the end of his last letter: BRING MRZZL FOR JURNEY. This was a British Railways regulation for dogs; and Ben had bought the muzzle out of his own money, and been proud to do so.

'For a very small dog,' he had said.

'Bad-tempered?' the shopman had asked sympathetically.

'No. Just fierce when provoked.'

Now, carrying all these things, he stepped out of the train at Castleford and there were his grand-father and Young Tilly waiting for him. No other dog; but his grandfather said at once: 'He's waiting at home for you.'

Nothing now – surely nothing – could go wrong.

Even the weather was perfect, and the hawthorn was already out along the driftway hedges as they walked up from where the Castleford bus had dropped them. The Fitches' little half-house was sunning itself, with the front door stopped open. Granny was sitting on a chair outside, very slowly shelling peas into a colander that glinted like silver in the sunshine.

'Well!' she said, as they came up; and almost at once

a dog began barking. Ben saw him come bounding out from behind the back of the house, barking jollily. He saw that he was large – almost as large as Tilly herself – and coloured a chestnut brown.

The dog saw Ben. He stopped. He stared at Ben; and Ben was already staring at him.

'He's not used to strangers up the driftway,' Grandpa said softly. 'He never sees 'em. He's a bit nervous – timid. Call him, Ben.' Then, after a pause: 'He's your dog: why don't you call him to you?'

Ben said: 'He's so big, and brown – I didn't expect it.'

'Call him.'

Ben wetted his lips, glanced sideways at his grandfather, and called: 'Chiquitito!' His tongue tripped over the syllables: the name turned out to be terribly difficult to call aloud.

The dog had taken a step or two backwards. Ben called again. The dog turned round altogether and fled round the corner of the house, out of sight.

'*What* did you call him?' asked Grandpa.

But Granny knew. 'Why do you call him after Willy's dog?'

Not after Willy's dog, but Ben's dog – the dog so small you could only see it with your eyes shut: the minute, fawn-coloured, brave Chiquitito. 'Because he's going to be Chiquitito – he *is* Chiquitito.'

'He's Brown,' said Grandpa. 'You can't change a dog's name like that – it only confuses him. Besides,' – he used Ben's own emphasis – 'he *is* Brown. You can't change that any more than you can change his nature. Call him again, boy – call him Brown.'

But Ben's mouth had closed in a line of deep obstinacy.

CHAPTER 19

Brown

Chiquitito-Brown was playing with his liver-and-white sister, Tilda, from next door. They chased and pounced and barked in the Fitches' little front garden. Tilly, their mother, lay in the sun on the front doorstep, her forepaws crossed, watching. Whenever one of the young dogs flounced too near her, she grumbled in her throat.

'They get on her nerves nowadays,' said Grandpa, '– puppies of that size and spirit. They know she'll stand no nonsense from them, but sometimes they over-excite each other and then they forget. Then Till gives a nip or two, to remind 'em. She'll do much better when there's only one to manage – when Brown's gone.'

Ben and his grandparents had finished their dinner, and soon it would be time for Ben to take the afternoon bus back to Castleford. His grandfather was not accompanying him, but – of course – Chiquitito-Brown was. So far Ben had not spoken to his dog again, and had not even touched him. Gloomily, from the shadow of indoors, he had watched him playing in the sunlight with Tilda.

Now Grandpa called Chiquitito-Brown to him, and held him while he directed Ben to fasten the collar round the dog's neck. This was the first time that Chiquitito-Brown had felt a collar, and he hated it.

'You'll have to scratch his name and address on the plate as soon as you get home,' Grandpa said. 'Or you could do it here and now. It wouldn't take long for a boy with schooling to scratch "Brown –"'

'No,' said Ben 'not here and now.'

Then Grandpa held the dog by the collar, while Ben clipped on the lead and Chiquitito-Brown hated that too. He felt himself in captivity, and feared his captor – a stranger, whose voice and hands were without friendliness.

Ben, having said his good-byes, set off for the bus, but Chiquitito-Brown would go with him only by being dragged in a half-sitting position at the end of the lead. Tilly watched, unmoved; Tilda, in astonishment.

Grandpa called after them: 'Pick him up, boy, and carry him.' Ben muttered, but picked him up. The dog was heavy to carry, and he struggled; but Ben held him firmly, grimly. So they went down the driftway.

Granny shaded her eyes, looking after them.

'People get their heart's desire,' she said, 'and then they have to begin to learn how to live with it.'

The weather had been perfect in London, too: office-girls, blooming in coloured cotton dresses and white sandals, had eaten their mid-day sandwiches on park benches in the sun; City business men had ventured out for the whole day without umbrellas.

After her morning's housework, Mrs Blewitt had washed all the loose-covers, and pegged them out in the little back garden in the sun. Frankie and Paul had helped. Then it was dinner-time; and after that the two boys went out on to the Heath.

'Be sure you're back in good time for tea,' Mrs Blewitt told them. 'Remember, Ben will be bringing his dog; everyone will be here to see it.' Mr Blewitt would be back for tea, and May and Charlie and Dilys were calling in.

'We'll be back,' said Paul.

'We'll come back by the Tube-station,' said Frankie. 'We might meet him.'

They nearly did. Ben, coming out of the Tube station with the brown dog under his arm, saw the two of them peering into a sweet-shop window – they had been dawdling and window-gazing for nearly half an hour. He knew, as soon as he saw them, that he did not want to meet them; not with this dog.

He slipped quickly round a street-corner, out of sight. Then he set the dog on the pavement, with the dry remark, 'We can both walk now.' But where? He did not want to go home – not with this dog.

The brown dog dragged reluctantly at the end of the lead as Ben went up the asphalted way to Parliament Hill. On the top, Ben stopped and unfastened the lead. He felt a bitter relief that he was free of the dog now. He gave it a push: 'Go away then, you! Go!'

The brown dog, nameless because no longer named, moved away a little and then sat down. Ben tried to shoo him, but he simply moved out of reach and sat down again. Then Ben set off angrily over the Heath; the brown dog got up and followed him at a little distance. He knew by now that Ben did not want him, and so he did not really want Ben; but Ben was all he had. So the two of them went across the Heath, together but not in companionship.

Ben walked steadily, but he had neither destination nor purpose. He walked away the worst of his anger, and also what was left of the afternoon. There had been a good many people on the Heath when he first came, but now they were going home. It was late for their teas, or even time for their suppers.

He topped a rise and saw the landmark of the flag-staff by the pond. It was flying the Union Jack, and he remembered what the keeper had said: that the Union Jack was flown only to celebrate special days. Perhaps this was a royal birthday; but, seeing the flag, Ben was reminded that this was to have been a day of celebration for him. This was the wonderful day when he got his dog. As he gazed, the flag of joy began to descend. A keeper was lowering it: he detached it altogether, furled it, and carried it off; and that was that. Ben turned abruptly back over the Heath.

The flag on Hampstead Heath – Union Jack or L.C.C. house-flag – is run down at sunset. The people who had not been drawn home to teas and suppers were now leaving the Heath because of chilliness and the fall of evening. Only Ben wandered farther and farther over the Heath; and the brown dog still followed him, but at a greater distance now, more laggingly.

There was solitude, stillness of evening, dusk that was turning the distant trees from green to black ... Ben slowed his pace; he sat down on a slope commanding a wide expanse. He was alone on the Heath now, except for the brown dog. The dog had sat down in the middle distance and was gazing at Ben.

Ben knew that, if he called the dog by the name he was used to, he would surely come; but Ben did not call him. And if he never called him, in time the dog would get up and wander away. He would be lost on Hampstead Heath – a nameless, ownerless, brown puppy-dog for some policeman to take in charge at last.

Did Ben care? He remembered his shame on the bus, when the brown dog sat trembling on his knee and the conductress had said, 'He needs a bit of cuddling; he's scared to death.' He remembered taking the dog into the guard's-van of the train at Castleford: he had been about to put on the muzzle, according to regulations, when the guard had said, 'Don't you bother with that. The animal looks more afraid of being bitten than likely to bite.' Ben had been humiliated; for the whole journey he sat at a distance, on a crate of chickens, his face turned away from the dog. Their arrival at Liverpool Street Station, the escalators, the Tube train – all of London that this dog first encountered terrified him. Ben had had to carry that heavy, trembling weight everywhere. He did so without tenderness or pity. He felt a disappointment that was cruel to him and made him cruel.

No Chiquitito . . . Ben let his head fall forward upon his knees and wept for that minute, intrepid, fawn-coloured dog that he could not have. Other people had the dogs they wanted: the Codling boy and the Russian huntsmen and people he had seen on the Heath this very afternoon – and, long ago, in Mexico, the little girl in the white dress with long, white, ribboned sleeves.

But Ben – no Chiquitito . . .

He shut his eyes tight, but he could see no invisible dog nowadays. He opened his eyes, and for a moment he could see no visible dog either. So the brown dog had gone at last. Then, as Ben's eyes accustomed themselves to the failing light, he could pick him out after all, by his movement: the dog had got up; he was moving away; he was slipping out of sight.

Then, suddenly, when Ben could hardly see, he saw clearly. He saw clearly that you couldn't have impossible things, however much you wanted them. He saw that if you didn't have the possible things, then you had nothing. At the same time Ben remembered other things about the brown dog besides its unChiquitito-like size and colour and timidity. He remembered the warmth of the dog's body against his own, as he had carried him; and the movement of his body as he breathed; and the tickle of his curly hair; and the way the dog had pressed up to him for protection and had followed him even in hopelessness.

The brown dog had gone farther off now, losing himself in dusk. Ben could not see him any longer. He stood up; he peered over the Heath. No . . .

Suddenly knowing what he had lost – *whom* he had lost, Ben shouted, 'Brown!'

He heard the dog's answering barks, even before he could see him. The dog was galloping towards him out of the dusk, but Ben went on calling: 'BrownBrownBrownBrown!'

Brown dashed up to him, barking so shrilly that Ben had to crouch down and, with the dog's tongue slapping all over his face, put his arms round him and said steadyingly, 'It's all right, Brown! Quiet, quiet! I'm here!'

Then Ben stood up again, and Brown remained by

his side, leaning against his leg, panting, loving him; and lovingly Ben said, 'It's late, Brown. Let's go home.'

AFTERWORD

Books, like dreams, linger in the memory. If you have read *A Dog So Small* with pleasure you will probably find one day that, seeing an old man walking his dog, you'll think with affection of Ben's wily and loyal grandfather. Or a pigeon on the window-sill may put you in mind of Ben's tenth birthday, the morning when his hopes of getting a dog as a birthday present were dashed. That, as you will remember, was the beginning of his obsession – it was more than a dream really – with 'a dog so small he could only see it with his eyes shut'.

Ben is a quiet kind of boy, not the kind that would go stomping around saying, 'I WANT A DOG', but the kind who hopes for a dog, dreams about dogs of all shapes and sizes in bizarre situations. The author has therefore made the book about him a quiet kind of book, a book that belongs to the reader personally.

When Philippa Pearce first wrote *A Dog So Small* – after she had won the Carnegie Medal for *Tom's Midnight Garden* – she sent it to her usual publisher. But this publisher decided not to publish it, wondering perhaps whether children would read a story that had no villains in it and no wild adventures. *A Dog So Small* is about the inner life of a boy, an inner life that is more real to him than the rumbustious life that is going on around him in the Blewitt household.

At that time I happened to be working for another publisher. When Philippa Pearce offered the manuscript of *A Dog So Small* to this publisher it was read by several of us and admired for the way the story is told – slowly, making the reader wait almost as impatiently as Ben for the next twist and the next, in what is really a very simple tale. It was admired, too, for the subtle way we readers get to know all the characters through their conversations with one another. But like the first publisher to whom it had been sent, we asked ourselves whether it was a book *children* would take to.

There was only one way to find out: give it to a nine-year-old boy to read. The nine-year-old boy was my cousin Charlie, who was, like you, a good reader. Also like you all, in all probability, Charlie had never tried to read a 'book' that was only, at that stage, an untidy heap of typed-on paper with (of course) none of the line drawings that now illustrate the story so well.

Charlie agreed to read the manuscript of *A Dog So Small*. We didn't ask him to write a report on the story – we already knew that as a piece of literature (though perhaps for adults?) it was a small gem. What we wanted to know was how Charlie had *felt* about it as he read. When he had turned the last sheet of typing paper and knew that Ben and Brown had finally found one another, Charlie wrote: 'I loved the story, but I'm not sure if I'll tell my friends, because I don't want to have to talk about it with anyone.'

Charlie had hit the nail on the head. Since he read the manuscript of *A Dog So Small*, over thirty years ago now, thousands of children have read the book and loved it, *privately*.

If you are one of those, you may go on to read Philippa Pearce's *The Minnow On the Say* and *Tom's Midnight Garden*. *The Minnow On the Say* is an adventure story in which two boys, paddling their canoe, the *Minnow*, up and down the River Say, turn amateur detective; in *Tom's Midnight Garden*, when the old clock strikes at midnight, Tom travels back in time to meet the people who lived in the house in which he is staying whilst in quarantine for measles. In both these stories you will be delighted to find yourself once again in the same part of England – Little Barley and Castleford – that Ben visits in *A Dog So Small*. Little Barley and Castleford are the names the author has invented for a village and town in the part of Cambridgeshire where she now lives, in a cottage close to the house where she was born.

Elaine Moss

Some other Puffin Modern Classics

THE BORROWERS
Mary Norton

CARRIE'S WAR
Nina Bawden

CHARLOTTE'S WEB
E. B. White

THE CHILDREN OF GREEN KNOWE
Lucy Boston

THE DARK IS RISING
Susan Cooper

THE FRIENDS
Rosa Guy

THE MOUSE AND HIS CHILD
Russell Hoban

MRS FRISBY AND THE RATS OF NIMH
Robert C. O'Brien

THE SILVER SWORD
Ian Serraillier

SMITH
Leon Garfield

STIG OF THE DUMP
Clive King

THE TURBULENT TERM OF TYKE TILER
Gene Kemp

TOM'S MIDNIGHT GARDEN
Philippa Pearce

WATERSHIP DOWN
Richard Adams

TOM'S MIDNIGHT GARDEN

Sent to stay with his aunt and uncle in a dull old house without even a garden, Tom is not looking forward to his summer holiday.

But when the clock strikes thirteen at midnight, Tom opens a door to find an adventure more wonderful than he could ever have imagined.

CARRIE'S WAR
Nina Bawden

Evacuated from London to Wales during the Second World War, Carrie and her brother are sent to live with the very strict Mr Evans.

But in trying to heal the breach between Mr Evans and his estranged sister, Carrie does the worst thing she ever did in her life.

THE CHILDREN OF GREEN KNOWE
Lucy Boston

Tolly isn't looking forward to spending Christmas with his great-grandmother in her strange house, but as soon as he arrives at Green Knowe he is delighted by the very special kind of magic he finds all around him.

Indeed, far from being lonely, Tolly is caught up in a wonderful adventure with the other children who have lived there, eagerly learning all about the mysterious house and its delightful secrets.

GOODNIGHT MISTER TOM
Michelle Magorian

Young Willie Beech is evacuated to the country as Britain stands on the brink of the Second World War. A sad, deprived child, he slowly begins to flourish under the care of old Tom Oakley – but his new-found happiness is shattered by a summons from his mother back in London . . .

Winner of the *Guardian* Children's Fiction Prize.

TARKA THE OTTER
Henry Williamson

This classic story of an otter's life and death in the Devon countryside captures the feel of nature and wildlife as though it is seen through his eyes.

Its atmosphere and detail make it easy to see why Tarka has become one of the best-loved creatures in world literature.

THE BORROWERS
Mary Norton

Pod, Homily and Arrietty are a family of tiny people who live beneath the floor, behind the kitchen clock. Everything they have is borrowed from the 'human beans' who don't even know they exist.

That is, until the fateful day when Arrietty makes friends with 'the boy upstairs'.

WATERSHIP DOWN
Richard Adams

Fiver felt sure that something terrible was going to happen to the warren – and Fiver's sixth sense was never wrong.

Yet the fleeing band of rabbits could never have imagined the terrors and dangers they were to encounter in their search for a new home.